Skills Development
for
Rugby League

JOHN KEAR

Queen Anne Press

A QUEEN ANNE PRESS BOOK

© The Rugby Football League, 1996

First published in 1996 by
Queen Anne Press
a division of
Lennard Associates
Mackerye End
Harpenden
Herts AL5 5DR

A catalogue entry is available from the British Library.

ISBN 1 85291 573 0

Cover design: Paul Cooper
Design Consultants: Design 2 Print
Editor: Neil Tunnicliffe
Production Editor: Chris Hawkes
Origination: Leaside Graphics
Printed and bound in Great Britain by
Ebenezer Baylis, Worcester

CONTENTS

ACKNOWLEDGEMENTS

My thanks go to all the many people who have made this publication possible. I should particularly like to thank the players whom I have been involved with since starting my coaching career at Castleford in the mid-1980s and the many coaches whom I have worked alongside in that period. Particular mention must be made of the biggest influence on my coaching career to this moment in time, the previous Rugby Football League Director of Coaching, Phil Larder, who has proved an inspiration to many coaches at all levels, myself included.

It has also been a privilege to work alongside such great coaches as Malcolm Reilly and Darryl Van de Velde, who have been instrumental in my development.

I should also like to thank the many coaches who have passed through the coaching system for their ideas and inspiration; the staff coaches of the British Rugby League Coaching Scheme, Warren Ayres, John Bartlett, Garth Budge, Dave Busfield, Howard Cartwright, Neil Harrison, Paul Johnstone, Denis McHugh, Ted McNamara, Frank Punchard, Rick Rolt, Danny Sheehy, Steve Wood, Simon Worsnop, David Ward, Dave Wright, Eric Fitzsimons, Clive Griffiths, Arthur Keegan and Graham Starkey; the Development Officers based at the Rugby Football League, Andy Harland, Garry Schubert, Nigel Johnston, Mike Rowan, Damian McGrath, Tony Rea, Steve Rosolen, Michael Hogan, Dave Evans, Stewart Williams, Ralph Rimmer, Martyn Ward, Kevin Tamati and Ray Unsworth; and also the head coaches at professional clubs.

My thanks go also to Maurice Lindsay and his Board of Directors at the Rugby Football League, Neil Tunnicliffe, Project Co-ordinator at the Rugby Football League, and to Sue Bowden, Coaching Secretary at the Rugby Football League.

Furthermore, it would be remiss of me not to pay tribute to the many people from Australia such as Shaun McRae and Frank Ponnissi, who sat through many hours of discussions about skills related work and its use in the development of a Rugby League player.

All the photographs in this book are published by kind permission of the Varley Wilkinson Photograph Agency.

The purpose of this book is to build upon the foundations laid by the *Rugby League Coaching Manual* by Phil Larder, first published in 1988 with an updated second edition in 1992 which was accepted throughout the sporting world as a first-class guide to coaching the game of Rugby League.

This new book is now one of the official set texts for the British Rugby League Coaching Scheme courses which run over four levels from beginners to elite performers. The book is based upon the skill drills and the small-sided games that form the core of these courses. However, many new activities are also incorporated to further develop the skills required for Rugby League.

Wherever coaching sessions are observed, the leader is always asked afterwards to explain this drill or that game. This text serves as a reference point for those open minded individuals who wish to add variety to coaching sessions or develop a skill in a different way. It is intended that these extensive practices, covering all aspects of individual and unit skill development within Rugby League, should be used as the basis for structured skill development programmes at all levels of the game.

It is essential that in today's high speed intense collision sport of Rugby League skills work is an integral part of coaching sessions so that players develop the necessary abilities to cope with the demands of the modern game.

The text serves as a technical reference point for the skills of Rugby League and a source of ideas to aid the development of these skills.

As an introduction to each set of practical activities, explanations of the relevance of the skills and coaching points are provided for the user. There then follows a set format to explain these activities. The activity is given a relevant title. There then follows a brief summary of the main skills developed through the activity with an approximation of the level of performer it is designed for. A concise explanation with diagram (if applicable) is then provided so that the drill or game can be set up quickly and efficiently and is easy to understand for the user. The final subtitle is for variations and progressions which allow the drill/game to be adapted so, in essence, the user is getting several activities out of the one drill/game. At the side of the page (where applicable), Level 1,2 or 3 will be seen. This relates to the coaching course that this drill/game is used upon.

Furthermore, it is hoped that from using this book the coach will be able to adapt, vary and invent activities specifically for his team's use. In order to do this all the coach needs to understand is that any activities can be made easier/more difficult by modifying the numbers involved and the area used. Another variable, pressure during activities, can be increased if the time element is reduced and opposition is introduced.

If one considers that it is obviously easiest to perform a skill against no opposition; the next step would be to provide passive opposition, then to use coaching aids such as shields so that the element of collision is introduced, before progressing to conditioned collision and finally match day pressure via fully fledged opposition.

Obviously it is your decision as a coach in respect of the ability of the performers in your care as to where to start the skills development and where you progress to at any given time, but anyone wishing to develop skill should use the activities in the book and then adapt and invent in order to get the most out of the players.

In summary, in order to develop skill, the following model should be used:

a) Brief introduction of the skill

b) Technically accurate visual demonstration

c) Relevant drill (skills activity)

d) Group feedback to reinforce coaching points or introduce new points

e) Further relevant skills activity

f) Individual feedback during activity

From the above it is obvious that the successful skills coach:

i) Requires the necessary knowledge (coaching points)

ii) Needs to be able to organise relevant practices

iii) Can stand back, observe and analyse the group as a whole and the players as individuals and

iv) Can communicate with the players so as to provide relevant feedback in order to improve their skill level.

In conclusion it is not enough simply to set up a drill or a game; it is essential that the coach uses this activity in order to improve performance. The drill/game is simply a means by which quality coaching can take place.

Remember the performer perfects what he practises: if he practises poor technique he will learn poor technique and have skill deficiencies. Therefore, 'perfect practise' is what the players require and what the coach has a duty to provide. Only then will the following ring true, 'PERFECT PRACTICE MAKES PERFECT'.

Please note that all male/female distinctions have been dropped in the text. Whilst recognising that large numbers of women and girls now play Rugby League, for the sake of brevity the word 'his' has been universally used instead of 'his/her'.

Travel of player with ball	———————▶
Travel of player without ball	▬ ▬ ▬ ▶
Travel of ball	• • • • • • • • ▶
Player	A, B, C etc or 1, 2, 3 etc
Attacker	A
Defender	D
Coach	C
Ball	⬮
Direction of movement	═══════▶
Marker cone	▲
Hit/tackle shield	▭
Tackle bag	▯
Play the ball	⊤

In order to utilise fully the technical information on drills and games contained in this text, it is important to understand the importance of skill to the player and its part within the game. If any coach was asked to list the essentials of a player, skill would be somewhere in that list. Therefore, it is an ingredient that a player cannot prosper without. However, a player who can simply perform Rugby League techniques in a training environment is not a skilled individual.

A skilled performer must have the correct mental attitude and determination to play Rugby League and be able to perform skills under match day pressure. The coach must realise that it is far easier to catch a high ball without opposition than to catch one which:

a) has been kicked high into the floodlights;

b) is coming down close to the goal posts;

c) is being chased by opponents who are onside and who will arrive at the same time as the ball.

A player who can do the former, i.e., catch a high ball without opposition, requires progressive practices to prepare him to become competent at the latter, i.e., catching a high ball under match day pressure.

The coach must recognise these facts and structure drills and games accordingly.

It could be suggested that a skilled performer is one who can perform the necessary skills against determined opposition. This is not entirely true. For example, a centre with an unmarked winger running outside him runs towards the touchline and switches the winger into the covering loose forward with a drop-off pass, that drop off may be executed perfectly technically, but the centre is not a skilled performer; he has performed the skill of the drop-off pass technically correctly, but it was the wrong skill at that moment in time. Skills, therefore, must be linked to thinking and the making of correct decisions. A skilled performer is one who can:

a) perform the techniques perfectly;

b) perform those techniques against opposition (under match day pressure);

c) decide correctly at any given moment which technique to perform.

It is hoped that the drills and the games contained in this book allow the performer to progress in a structured, rational way in order to develop a skill fully so that he becomes technically competent against intense opposition and can make the correct decision at the correct time.

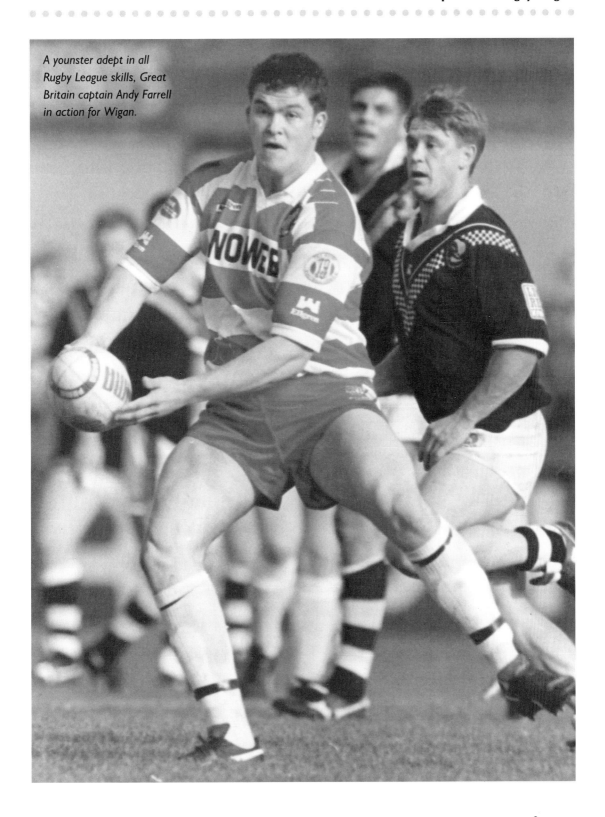

A younster adept in all Rugby League skills, Great Britain captain Andy Farrell in action for Wigan.

PASSING AND HANDLING

In Rugby League one of the fundamental principles of play is to control the ball. If a team of players are able to control possession that team will be a successful team. Individually, if a player can control possession, he will be a very successful player.

Rugby League, by its very nature, encourages all players to be good handlers of the ball and they should be given every opportunity to improve their handling abilities at each practice session.

Players, when first introduced to Rugby League, should be given the opportunity to run with the ball many times.

Put the players in as many situations where they can handle a ball, get a feel for a rugby ball and run with a rugby ball as possible.

Players then need to become adept at the techniques of passing and handling very early in their development.

All players will need to become proficient in the techniques of catching and passing in both directions and work related to such techniques should be included in every coaching session. Perfecting the skills is an ongoing task; progression and revision are very important to their development.

Coaches of all age groups must maintain this emphasis on quality handling skills. Players cannot practise handling skills enough and, when practising, coaches should insist on perfection.

The following group of skill drills and small-sided games are designed in order to develop outstanding handling skills.

It is, therefore, essential that the coach not only provides the environment for this development but also knows what to look for.

A truly magnificent ball handler,
Bobbie Goulding of St. Helens and
Great Britain.

Also included in this section are many drills incorporating decision making and support play. This is essential in passing and handling drills and in small-sided games. For players to have success, it is the responsibility not only of the ball carrier to make decisions but also of the support players.

The support player must:

a) read the situation, i.e., the ball carrier and the defence;

b) communicate;

c) run the most efficient angle; and

d) time his run.

The ball carrier must:

a) have the technical ability to carry out the appropriate pass;

b) have developed a measure of efficient decision making, i.e., whether to pass, who to pass to, when to pass and how to pass.

In order to be successful at this, he must be constantly aware of the movements of the opponents' defensive line and of his own support.

HOLDING THE BALL

What to look for (Coaching Points)

1. The player should make a cradle with the hands, fingers outspread under the ball with the palms facing inwards. The thumbs are placed on the upper part of the ball to hold it in position.

2. Arms should be relaxed with elbows slightly bent and close to the side.

Ball familiarisation

Skills Developed   Ball familiarisation

Level   <u>Beginner</u>/Intermediate/Advanced/All

(Left) A ball each for youngsters is the ideal. Let them run with it and familiarise themselves with it. (Right) Note the similarities between the young player's one-handed ball control technique and that of Gary Mercer, the Leeds and New Zealand forward.

Explanation

In suitable area

One ball each

Each player does various basic familiarisation drills individually in his own space, such as:

    Throwing the ball into the air and catching it

    Moving the ball from one hand to the other

    Moving the ball around the body

    Moving the ball in and out of his legs

    Rolling the ball from one hand to the other

Variations and Progressions

i) Firstly do these practices static, then walking, then jogging and finally running.

Pairs passing

Skills Developed   Passing and handling
Decision making
Concentration
Ball familiarisation

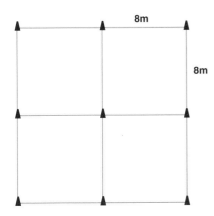

Level
<u>Beginner</u>/Intermediate/Advanced/All

Explanation

Grids are set out as shown.

Players are placed into pairs, one ball between two.

Players move freely around all four grids passing the ball between them.

The aim of the group is no dropped balls in a set time period.

The next stage is to reduce the area to two grids which increases difficulty before finally all players should be working in one grid.

Variations and Progressions

i) On the coach's command the player in possession should:

a) pass the ball around his body.

b) pass the ball through his legs.

c) tap the ball twice in the air.

d) roll the ball under control along the ground.

e) hold the ball in the correct passing position, i.e., the cradle, then pass to his partner.

Ball tag

Skills Developed   Evasion

Carrying the ball

Peripheral vision

Level   Beginner/Intermediate/Advanced/<u>All</u>

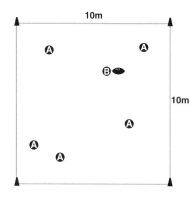

Explanation

Player B with the ball attempts to tag the A players with the ball. The ball must be held in two hands and be under control.

An A player who is tagged receives the ball and becomes the B player, the chaser.

Variations and Progressions

i) Underhand tagging only.

ii) Player B (chaser) has the ball for a set period of time and attempts as many tags as possible in that time.

iii) Place a tackle bag in the grid – no player is allowed to jump/straddle the bag.

iv) Extend to 3 v 3 so that the taggers have to pass the ball in order to 'corner' the evading team.

v) Extend to 4 grids. Runners can go anywhere but the 4 taggers (1 in each grid) must remain in their own grid.

Passing the Ball

What to look for (Coaching Points)

1. The player should hold the ball correctly.

2. Arms relaxed, elbows slightly bent.

3. Keep eyes on the target, i.e., the receiver's bread basket (between his lower chest and waist).

4. The trunk should be twisted at the hips so that the shoulders are square to the receiver.

5. The arms take the ball well back at the side of the hips.

6. The ball is aimed at the target (bread basket in front of the receiver).

7. The ball is passed with a straight trajectory and not lobbed.

8. The distance in front depends upon the speed of the receiver.

9. The ball is directed by the fingers and wrists.

10. There is a follow through with the arms so that finally they are fully extended towards the receiver with fingers pointing at the target.

NB Please ensure that the players practise passing to both left and right.

Catching the Ball

What to look for (Coaching Points)

1. Keep eyes on the ball all the way from the passer's hands.

2. Prepare to receive the ball with arms and fingers extended.

3. Twist the trunk to face the passer.

4. Use both hands whenever possible.

5. Bring the ball into the bread basket to make sure of possession, but then hold it in the hands ready to pass (do not cuddle it).

6. Be prepared to adjust the position of the body to receive a badly directed pass.

7. Be prepared for an unexpected pass as this is often the one which leads to a try.

8. Concentration is important.

9. Do not slacken speed when catching the ball.

Touch-down

Skills Developed   Handling, running with the ball and scoring a try.

Level   <u>Beginner</u>/<u>Intermediate</u>/Advanced/All

Explanation

Team A pass the ball up and down the line. On the command 'Go' (from the coach) the player in possession tries to run around his own team and ground the ball over the goal-line before being 'tackled' by the opposite player from Team B.

Team B player must run the same path as the ball carrier.

NB A two-handed touch, grip or an actual tackle is used depending on age or ability.

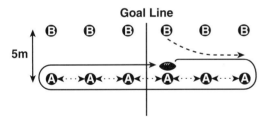

Levels 1 and 2

Stationary Passing in Pairs

Skills Developed   Passing

Level   Beginner/Intermediate/Advanced/All

Explanation

In pairs the players should pass to one another.

Vary the distances they are apart, ensuring that all passes are weighted correctly and that the trajectory of each pass is flat.

Variations and Progressions

Practise both to the left and right.

Passing Round the Grid

Skills Developed   Passing and handling

Level   Beginner/Intermediate/Advanced/All

Explanation

Player 1 starts with the ball, passes to 2, 2 to 3, 3 to 4, 4 to 1, etc. Ensure correct technique.

Variations and Progressions

i) Use both directions.

ii) Introduce competition to test mastery of technique.

iii) Turn the players so that they face the outside of the grid. This will encourage turning the body from receiving to passing.

Static Line Passing

Skills Developed   Passing and handling

Level   <u>Beginner</u>/Intermediate/Advanced/All

Explanation

Players line out as in diagram.

Player 1 starts with the ball, passes to 2, 2 to 3, 3 to 4.

Player 4 then passes back along the line.

Emphasise the fact that the upper body moves to face the passer before receiving. Upon receiving the ball the upper body turns to face the receiver.

3 v 1 Number of Passes

Skills Developed   Passing and handling

Decision making

Support play

Level   Beginner/Intermediate/Advanced/<u>All</u>

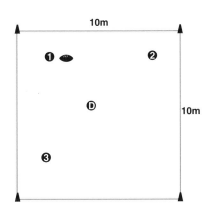

Explanation

Player 1 starts with the ball and he cannot run whilst in possession. He may pass to any team-mate (2 and 3) in any direction.

Defender (D) attempts to pressurise his three opponents into an error.

No body contact is allowed.

The ball carriers attempt to make 15 passes.

The support players may move freely.

Variations and Progressions

i) If skill level is low give the ball carriers further advantage by making the game 4 v 1.

ii) Passes can be restricted to 'Rugby League' passes only.

Level 2

4 v 4 Number of Passes

Skills Developed   Passing and handling

Decision making

Support play

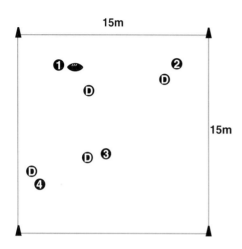

Level

Beginner/Intermediate/Advanced/<u>All</u>

Explanation

Player 1 starts with the ball and he cannot run whilst in possession.

He may pass to any team-mate (2, 3, and 4) in any direction. Defending team (D) attempt to pressure the ball handlers into an error.

No body contact is allowed.

The ball handlers attempt to make 15 consecutive passes. The support players may move freely.

Emphasise control of the ball.

Variations and Progressions

i) Passes can be restricted to 'Rugby League' passes only.

Marker Touch

Skills Developed   Passing and handling

Concentration

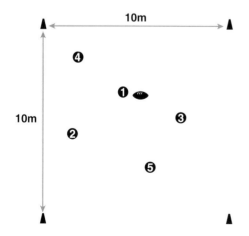

Level
<u>Beginner</u>/Intermediate/Advanced/All

Explanation

Player 1 starts with the ball and passes to any other player in the group. After he has passed the ball he touches any marker that forms the grid. The player who received the ball then passes to anyone in the group and touches any marker.

The drill is continuous.

Players must not touch the same cone twice consecutively, so promoting greater movement.

Variations and Progressions

i) Fewer players.

ii) More cones.

iii) More balls, players and cones.

'W' Pass

Skills Developed	Handling
	Concentration
Level	Beginner/Intermediate/Advanced/All

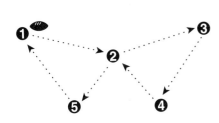

Explanation

The players are arranged in a 'W' formation, passing distance apart. The players remain stationary throughout the drill.

I starts with the ball, passes to 2, 2 to 3, 3 to 4, 4 to 2, 2 to 5, 5 to I and so on.

The ball is continually passed round the 'W' with pressure on No. 2.

After one minute change positions in 'W'.

Variations and Progressions

i) Introduction of a second ball.

Level 1

Union Jack

Skills Developed	Passing and handling
	Concentration
	Communication
Level	Beginner/Intermediate/Advanced/<u>All</u>

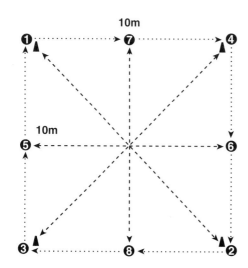

Explanation

Players 1 and 2 start with a ball each.

Player 1 passes to 7, 2 to 8.

Upon passing they interchange position.

7 then passes to 4, 8 passes to 3. 7 and 8 then interchange.

4 passes to 6, 3 to 5.

4 and 3 then interchange.

The drill then follows on continuously with the simple instructions to the players: catch, look, pass and change.

Variations and Progressions

i) Grid size may be increased and instead of one player on each side of the grid, a second may be incorporated.

Union Jack Extensions

Skills Developed	Passing and handling
	Communication
	Decision making
	Agility
Level	Beginner/Intermediate/Advanced/<u>All</u>

Explanation

Players commence as in diagram.

Players 1 and 7 start with a ball.

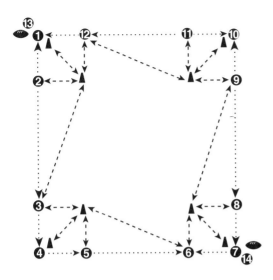

I passes to 2 and then advances to the nearest marker and retreats to 2's position.

2 passes to 3 and so on.

The same pattern is followed with the ball starting at Player 7 in the opposite corner.

NB i) always catch, look, pass, advance and then retreat in the same direction as you have passed.

ii) always have two players where the ball starts.

Variations and Progressions

i) After advancing to the cone, fall to the floor before retreating.

ii) Use 4 balls, i.e., ball at each corner but only advance to the nearest marker and then retreat to the same marker.

Straight/Diagonal

Skills Developed   Passing and handling
Angle of run
Concentration
Timing of run
Communication

Level   Beginner/Intermediate/Advanced/<u>All</u>

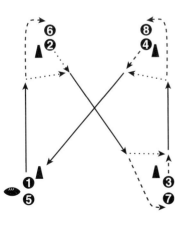

Explanation

Players start as shown in the diagram.

Player I starts with the ball and runs straight towards the top left hand marker. As he approaches the marker he passes to Player 2. I continues to behind Player 6.

On receiving the ball 2 runs diagonally to the bottom right hand marker. As he approaches the marker he passes to Player 3 and continues to behind Player 7.

3 receives and runs straight before passing to 4.

4 receives and runs diagonal before passing to 5.

The drill is continuous.

Variations and Progressions

i) More players and more balls.
ii) Drop off pass instead of a hand on.
iii) Mixture of drop off and hand on.

23

Octagon passing

Skills Developed   Passing and handling

Concentration

Level   Beginner/<u>Intermediate</u>/Advanced/All

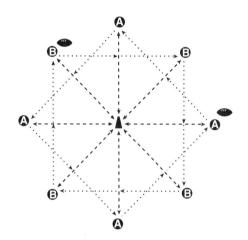

Explanation

Team A and Team B are set as shown.

Team B have one ball. Team A have one ball.

A players pass to A players one way. B players pass to B players the other way.

After a player has made a pass he runs forward to the marker in the middle and touches it before returning backwards to his original position.

Variations and Progressions

i) In 2 groups of 3 to put greatest pressure on the ball handlers.

ii) In 2 groups of 6 with 2 balls to each group.

Pop Up

Skills Developed   Passing and handling

Timing of run

Communication

Concentration

Level   Beginner/Intermediate/Advanced/<u>All</u>

Explanation

The players start as shown in the diagram. Player 1 has the ball and runs on the path as shown before popping a pass up to Player 2. 1 then goes to the back of Player 6. Upon receiving the ball 2 heads towards the next inner cone and pops a pass up to Player 3. 2 then goes behind Player 7. 3 receives and runs to the next inner cone before popping the ball up to 4 and so the drill continues.

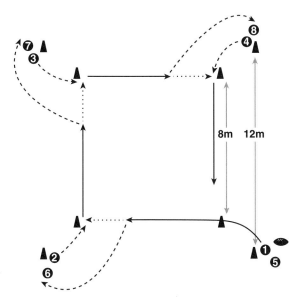

Variations and Progressions

i) Instead of a pop up pass a drop off can be introduced.

ii) A mixture of pop up then drop off can be used.

iii) For advanced players the ball carrier can communicate to the receiver either 'pop' or 'drop', so determining the type of pass.

iv) Additional balls can be introduced depending on the ability of the players.

Ball in the Air

Skills Developed

Handling

Concentration

Timing of run

Communication

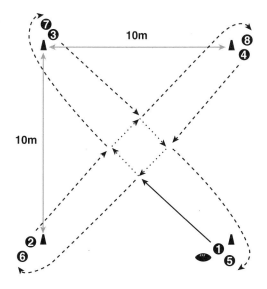

Level

Beginner/<u>Intermediate</u>/<u>Advanced</u>/All

Explanation

The players begin as in the diagram.

Player 1 starts with the ball, runs to the centre of the grid and pops the ball up into the air. He then angles off to join the line at the back of Player 6.

In the meantime Player 2 sets off at virtually the same time as Player 1, receives the ball and immediately pops it back into the air before joining the line at the back of Player 7.

3 then pops up to 4 and the drill continues. It must be stressed that the ball should always remain in the centre area and should be straight in and out of the hands.

Drop off, Hand on

Skills Developed	Passing and handling
	Timing of run

Level   Beginner/<u>Intermediate</u>/<u>Advanced</u>/All

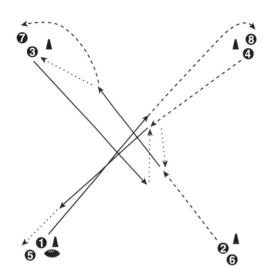

Explanation

Players start as shown in the diagram.

Player 1 starts with the ball and runs diagonally across the grid. Just after the mid point he does a drop off (switch) pass to Player 2 and then continues to join the line behind Player 8. Player 2 continues his run diagonally across the grid before passing to Player 3. 2 goes behind Player 7. 3 then runs diagonally across the grid and does a drop-off pass to 4 before going behind Player 6.

Player 4 continues his run diagonally across the grid before passing to Player 5. The whole sequence then continues.

Players always continue to the end of the line they are running towards.

Catch and Trail (1)

Skills Developed	Concentration
	Passing and handling
	Support play

Level   <u>Beginner</u>/<u>Intermediate</u>/Advanced/All

Explanation

Players are positioned as per the diagram. Player 1 starts with the ball, runs towards 2, passes to 2 and then remains at the marker. 3 has trailed behind 1. Player 2 on receiving the ball immediately passes to Player 3. 3 runs to 4, passes to him and then remains at the cone. 2 has trailed behind 3. 4 on receiving the ball

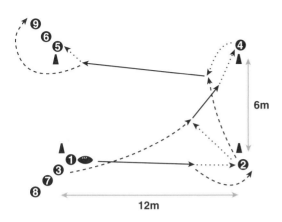

6m

12m

immediately passes to Player 2. 2 then runs to Player 5 and hands the ball on to him.

Player 5 then sets off with the ball with 6 trailing behind. They head toward Player 4. The first pattern is then run in reverse.

Variations and Progressions

i) See Catch and Trail (2)

Catch and Trail (2)

Skills Developed Concentration

Passing and handling

Support play

Level Beginner/Intermediate/<u>Advanced</u>/All

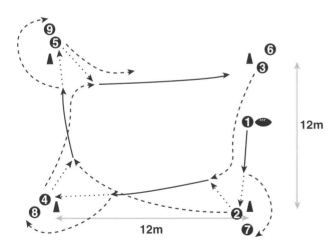

12m

12m

Explanation

The players are positioned as shown. Player 1 starts with the ball, runs towards Player 2, passes to 2 and joins the back of the line behind Player 7.

As soon as 1 sets off Player 3 trails behind him and receives the ball from 2. 3 runs to 4, passes to 4, and 2 trails 3 receiving the ball back from 4. 3 joins the line behind 8.

The drill is continuous.

Players on the marker simply go through the following: catch, pass, trail, receive, run and pass before joining the end of the line at the marker diagonally opposite.

Variations and Progressions

i) More players with up to 4 balls give a great deal of intensity. NB Build gradually to the 4-ball situation.

Receive and Trigger

Skills Developed   Concentration

                              Passing and handling

Level   Beginner/<u>Intermediate</u>/<u>Advanced</u>/All

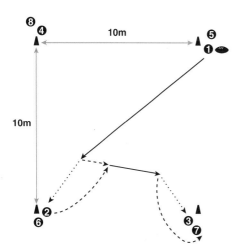

Explanation

Players are set out as in the diagram.

Player 1 starts with the ball, runs diagonally across the grid, passes to Player 2 who in turn returns the ball to Player 1, who then runs left and passes to Player 3. Player 1 then joins the back of that line.

The pattern is then repeated. Player 3 makes a diagonal run, passes to 4, receives the ball back, and continues left to Player 2 who is then 'triggered' off to run with the ball, and 3 joins the back of that line. The drill then continues as such.

Variations and Progressions

i) 12 players with a further ball or balls.

3 v 1 Invasion Game

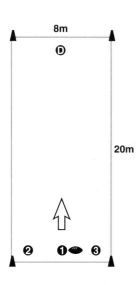

Skills Developed

Passing and handling

Decision making

Support play

Direct running

Level   Beginner/Intermediate/Advanced/<u>All</u>

Explanation

Ball-carrying team (players 1, 2 and 3) start with the ball and their aim is to carry the ball over the defenders' (D) goal-line which is at the far end of a corridor.

The ball carrier may run with the ball and should in fact be encouraged to do so.

The ball may be passed in any direction.

The defender attempts to stop the ball carriers with a two-handed touch, interception or by forcing an error.

Variations and Progressions

i) Condition the defender to advance as soon as the ball-carrying team does.

ii) Introduce three tackles so that if a ball carrier is 'tagged' a pass simply allows the attackers to recommence attacking for a total of three tackles.

PASSING BACKWARDS

What to look for (Coaching Points)

1. Run straight, attack the goal-line not the touchline.
2. Mobilise the upper body.
3. Pass accurately.
4. Look at the target area.
5. Weight the pass.
6. Direct the ball a suitable distance in front of the receiver.
7. Develop the ball carrier's awareness of the position of the support player.

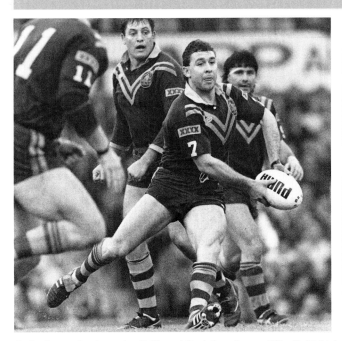 

Ricky Stuart for Australia (left) and Paul Broadbent of Sheffield (right) and England show classic passing technique emphasising all the coaching points on page 29.

Angled Line Passing

Skills Developed Passing and handling

Level Beginner/Intermediate/Advanced/All

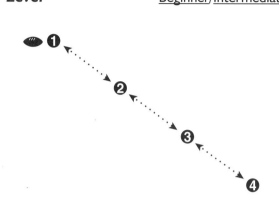

Explanation

Players line out as in diagram.

Player 1 starts with the ball, passes to 2, 2 to 3, 3 to 4.

All the players then turn about to face the opposite direction.

Player 4 then passes back along the line.

Ensure that each pass is made backwards.

Emphasise the fact that the legs and feet should be pointing directly downfield.

Variations and Progressions

i) Progress the practice to:

walking

jogging, and then

running.

Emphasise:

i) Line re-alignment by the receivers so that all passes are backward.

ii) Upper body turn.

Line Passing – Cone Opposition

Skills Developed   Passing and handling

Level   Beginner/<u>Intermediate</u>/Advanced/All

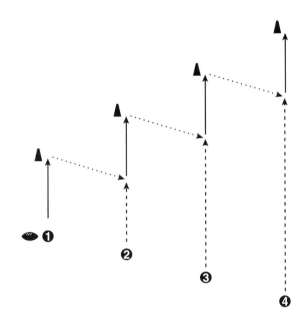

Explanation

Players start as in diagram.

Cones are set out as in diagram.

Player 1 starts with the ball and jogs to the first cone and passes to 2, 2 to 3, 3 to 4.

Begin with jogging and then increase speed as proficiency increases.

Emphasise awareness of the opposition as well as correct passing and receiving technique.

Encourage straight running.

Variations and Progressions

i) Move cones gradually until a flat defensive line is achieved.

ii) Replace cones with passive defenders.

iii) Replace passive defenders with defenders with shields.

iv) Defenders to walk forward.

v) More than one line of cones, etc, can be used to encourage pass and re-align to support.

Continuous Line Passing

Skills Developed   Passing and handling

Line alignment

Concentration

Level   Beginner/Intermediate/Advanced/<u>All</u>

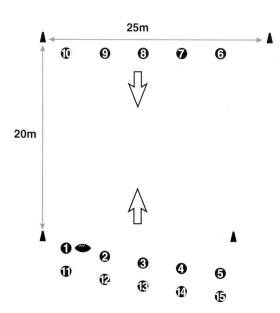

Explanation

Player 1 starts with the ball and the line (Players 1 to 5) begin advancing to the far side of the grid.

Player 1 then passes to 2, who passes to 3, 3 to 4 and 4 to 5. All passes should be as per Rugby League laws.

Player 5 on receiving the ball then pops a pass up to Player 6 and the line (Players 6 to 10) begins advancing and passing the ball until it reaches Player 10 who pops the ball up for Player 11.

The drill continues for a set time.

Variations and Progressions

i) Different types of passes and angles of run can be incorporated:

a) Player 1 passes to 2, 2 then drops off 3 who links with 4 and 5 before handing on to Player 6 – each line runs similar patterns.

b) Player 1 passes to 2, 2 then throws a long pass to miss out 3 and pick up Player 4 who links with 5 before handing on to Player 6 and so on.

There are many patterns that can be run according to the player's ability.

Line Turnover

Skills Developed

Line passing and handling

Concentration

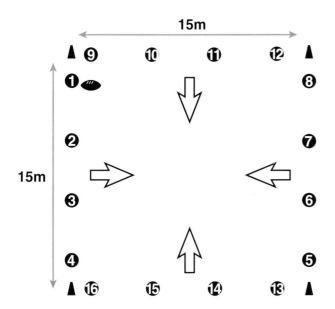

Level

Beginner/<u>Intermediate</u>/Advanced/All

Explanation

Players begin as in diagram.

Player 1 starts with the ball. Players 1 to 4 begin crossing the grid, 1 passes to 2, to 3 and finally to 4.

4 then hands on to Player 5.

Players 5 to 8 then begin crossing the grid, 5 passes to 6, to 7 and finally to 8.

8 then passes to Player 9.

Players 9 to 12 begin crossing the grid, 9 passes to 10, to 11 and finally to 12.

12 then hands on to Player 13.

Players 13 to 16 then begin crossing the grid, 13 passes to 14, to 15 and finally to 16.

The drill then continues as above.

Wave Passing

Level 3

Skills Developed   Long passing

Support play

Level   Beginner/Intermediate/<u>Advanced</u>/All

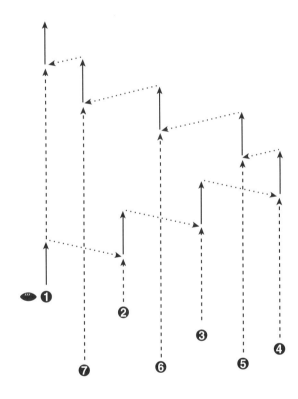

Explanation

The players commence as shown.

Player 1 makes a long pass to 2, 2 to 3, 3 to 4.

Player 4 then gives a short pass to Player 5 who brings his wave of support to the front.

Then 5 long passes to 6, 6 to 7.

Player 7 then gives a short pass to Player 1.

The drill continues.

Variations and Progressions

i) Combinations of long and short passes.

ii) Combine single file passing drill and the players, on a given command, fan out across the field and the ball is moved wide.

Feed and Receive

Skills Developed   Line passing

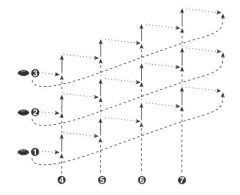

Level   Beginner/<u>Intermediate</u>/<u>Advanced</u>/All

Explanation

Players commence as shown.

Players 1, 2 and 3 are the feeders.

Player 1 passes to Player 4, 4 to 5, 5 to 6, 6 to 7 and back to Player 1 who has looped around the advancing line of Players 4 to 7.

Player 2 repeats this process as does Player 3.

Channel Drill

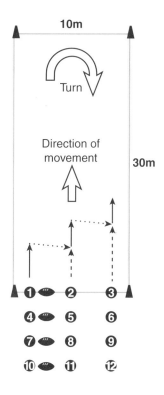

Skills Developed

Passing and handling

Decision making

Line alignment

Level   Beginner/<u>Intermediate</u>/<u>Advanced</u>/All

Explanation

In groups of 3, a ball to each group.

Players 1 to 3 advance down the channel interpassing. Upon reaching the end of the channel they immediately turn and return the opposite way still interpassing.

Groups 4 to 6, 7 to 9 and 10 to 12 are set off at regular spaced intervals following the same procedure.

Variations and Progressions

i) Size of channel and number of players.

Pass and Position

Skills Developed   Passing and handling

Re-alignment

Concentration

Level   Beginner/<u>Intermediate</u>/Advanced/All

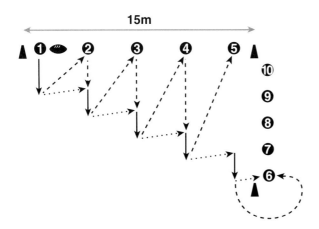

Explanation

Players begin as shown in the diagram.

Players 1 to 5 begin moving as an attacking line. 1 has the ball, passes to 2 then slides back into 2's original position.

2 receives, passes to 3 then slides back into 3's original position.

This is repeated until the pass reaches 5.

Player 5 then passes to 6 and takes up his position.

Players 6 to 10 then repeat the above passing and sliding movements with 10 taking the end position.

The drill is continuous with players working themselves along the positions.

Three Lines Pass

Skills Developed   Lateral passing and handling

Timing of run

Communication

Level   <u>Beginner</u>/<u>Intermediate</u>/Advanced/All

Explanation

Player 1 starts with the ball, runs forward and passes to Player 2, who has advanced from his starting marker, receives the ball and passes to Player 3.

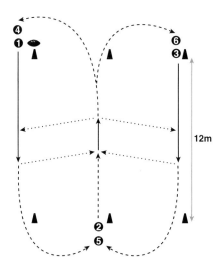

12m

3 then passes to 5, 5 to 4 and so on.

The drill is continuous provided the players always join the back of the line from where they have received the pass.

Variations and Progressions

i) Widen the passing distance.

ii) Shorten the running distance.

Both of these progressions lead to greater pressure on the passer.

Grid Support

Skills Developed   Passing and handling

Support play

Concentration

Communication

Level   Beginner/Intermediate/<u>Advanced</u>/All

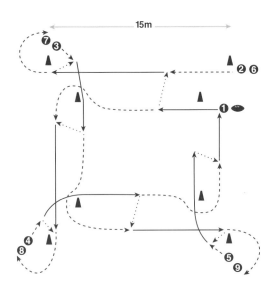

Explanation

Players begin as shown in the diagram.

1 and 2 begin running at the same time, Player 1 in possession of the ball.

1 passes to 2.

2 carries the ball, drops off Player 3 and joins the line at the back of Player 7.

3 receives the drop off, runs to the left of the inside cone before straightening up and passing to Player 1 who has rounded the cone and followed 3.

1 continues down his straight path with the ball, drops off Player 4 and joins the line at the back of Player 8.

4 receives the drop off, runs to the left of the inside cone before straightening and passing to Player 3 who has rounded the cone and followed 4.

3 continues down his straight path with the ball, drops off Player 5 and joins the line at the back of Player 9.

The drill then continues as such.

Variations and Progressions

i) More players and additional balls (only at a very advanced stage).

Pressure Pass

Skills Developed

Passing and handling

Concentration

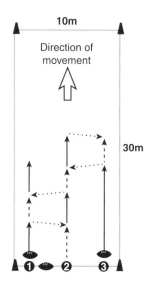

Level

Beginner/<u>Intermediate</u>/<u>Advanced</u>/All

Explanation

Players begin at one end of the corridor. Players 1 and 3 start with a ball each.

The players begin going along the length of the corridor.

Player 1 passes to 2, 2 then returns ball to 1, Player 3 then passes to 2, 2 back to 3.

Player 1 to 2, 2 back to 1 and so on. Always insist on passing within the rules.

Arrowhead

Skills Developed

Passing and handling

Concentration

Line alignment

Level

Beginner/<u>Intermediate</u>/<u>Advanced</u>/All

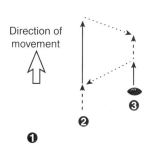

Explanation

Players line up in arrowhead formation, passing distance apart. Player 3 starts with the ball.

The group advances downfield. 3 passes to 2 who in turn passes back to 3. Player 2 then runs around to the outside of Player 5.

In the meantime, 3 passes to 4 who passes back to 3 before running to the outside of Player 1.

The drill then continues as above. Ensure that all passes are within the rules.

2 v 1 Lateral

Skills Developed　　Passing and handling

Support play

Decision making

Communication

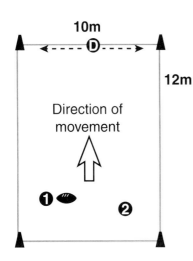

10m

12m

Direction of
movement

Level

Beginner/Intermediate/Advanced/<u>All</u>

Explanation

Players 1 and 2 attempt to beat the defender.
The defender can only move laterally.
He is not allowed to advance at all.

Variations and Progressions

l) Different offensive and defensive numbers pose different
problems, e.g., 3 v 1, 3 v 2, 4 v 2.

ii) Attack a corridor of grids with defenders spaced along them.

2 v 1

Skills Developed　　Passing and handling
Support play
Decision making
Communication

Level　　Beginner/Intermediate/Advanced/<u>All</u>

Explanation

Players1 and 2 attempt to beat the defender. Ensure that all three situations in the diagrams are practised, i.e.,

i) defender diagonally opposite the ball carrier.

ii) defender in the middle of the grid.

iii) defender in line with the ball carrier.

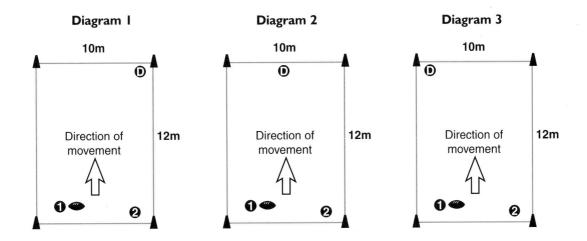

Diagram 1	Diagram 2	Diagram 3

Variations and Progressions

i) Condition the reactions of the defender.

ii) Allow defender free rein.

iii) Defender carries tackle shield.

iv) Attack down a corridor of grids with defenders spaced along them.

2 v 1 Continuous

Skills Developed	Decision making
	Handling
	Support play
	Communication

Level   Beginner/Intermediate/Advanced/<u>All</u>

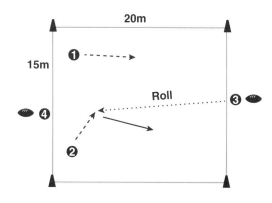

Explanation

Player 3 rolls ball towards Players 1 and 2. Player 1 or 2 picks the ball up and both 1 and 2 attack the goal-line defended by Player 3. Player 3 only comes 'alive' as a defender when one of the attackers picks up the ball. Upon scoring a try or an error Player 4 starts the process again with 1 and 2 trying to score past him.

Player 3 retrieves the other ball to keep the 2 v 1 process continuous.

NB i) Two-handed touch by grip to be used by the defender.

ii) Set a period of time for the attackers to work before changing position.

Variations and Progressions

i) Can be passed from defenders (Players 3 and 4).

ii) Can be grubber or chip kicked from defenders.

iii) Can be extended to 3 v 2, 4 v 2 etc.

2 v 1 Alternate

Skills Developed	Passing and handling
	Decision making
	Support play
	Timing of run

Level   Beginner/<u>Intermediate</u>/<u>Advanced</u>/All

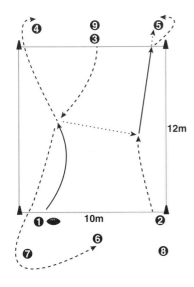

Explanation

Player 1 starts with the ball and attacks the far grid-line along with Player 2. As soon as 1 advances Player 3 becomes alive as a defender.

This creates a 2 v 1 situation and if done correctly Player 2 will 'score' at the far end of the grid.

Upon getting to the far end 2 simply hands the ball on to Player 5.

Players 5 and 4 now become the 2 attackers against Player 6 defending. The drill continues with players alternating roles at each end.

Variations and Progressions

i) Condition the defender as to where he can start in relation to the ball carrier

2 v 1 Through the Gate

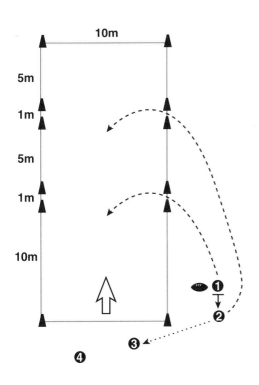

Skills Developed

Passing and handling
Decision making
Support play

Level

Beginner/<u>Intermediate</u>/<u>Advanced</u>/All

Explanation

Players begin as shown.

Player 1 starts with the ball and plays it in the correct manner to Player 2. 1 then sprints to the first 'gate' and becomes an active defender.

Player 2 then passes to Player 3. Upon passing, 2 sprints to the second 'gate' and becomes an active defender.

When Player 3 receives the ball from 2, Players 3 and 4 become 'line' attackers progressing along the corridor in the direction shown.

Two-handed touch is used.

Variations and Progressions

i) When the defenders go through the gate, they can only move laterally and not advance towards the two attackers.

ii) A tackle shield is placed at the 'gate' entrance to allow game related contact.

2 v 1 + 1

Skills Developed

Passing and handling

Decision making

Support play

Level

Beginner/<u>Intermediate</u>/<u>Advanced</u>/All

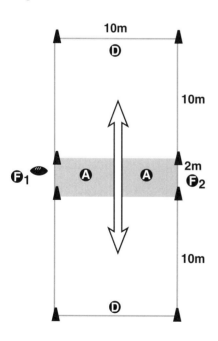

Explanation

The players start as shown in the diagram.

Feeder 1 (F1) passes the ball to an attacker (A) who attacks one of the two defenders (D).

A 2 v 1 situation is naturally created.

The defender can only advance when the attackers have cleared the shaded neutral zone. He endeavours to prevent a try being scored by a two-handed touch, an interception or forcing an error.

Once a try has been scored or a breakdown in play occurs, i.e., touch or an error, the attackers turn around, receive a ball from F2 and begin attacking the other end of the grids.

The other defender then comes into play once the attackers come out of the neutral zone.

This is a continuous drill limited by a set number of attacks, e.g., 10, or a time limit, e.g., 1 minute.

NB It is important that the two feeders maintain a constant availability of balls.

Variations and Progressions

i) Defenders are conditioned to move laterally only.

ii) The ball is rolled into the neutral zone for the attackers to pick up.

iii) The attackers are allowed up to six tackles (touches) to score and the ball is brought back into play via a pass.

iv) Size of area is adjusted and numbers are e.g., 3 v 1 + 1 or 4 v 2 + 2.

3 v 2

Skills Developed

Passing and handling

Support play

Communication

Decision making

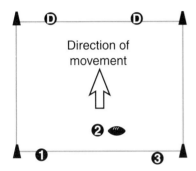

Direction of movement

Level Beginner/<u>Intermediate</u>/<u>Advanced</u>/All

Explanation

Players 1 to 3 attack the two defenders.

The ball carrier should be the middle man.

It is essential that he attacks the gap between the two defenders.

As the defenders react, the ball carrier should make the appropriate decision as to which support player to pass to.

Variations and Progressions

i) Condition the defenders' movement and/or decision making.

ii) Have the ball carrier start at the end and encourage the defenders to ensure all possible solutions – quick hands, early ball to the middle man and a face pass directly to the end man, are used.

iii) Have the defenders start close together and/or one behind the other.

iv) Attack down a corridor of grids with defenders spaced along them.

Level 3

3 v 1 Pressure Corridor

Skills Developed

Passing and handling

Support play

Decision making

Communication

Level

Beginner/<u>Intermediate</u>/<u>Advanced</u>/All

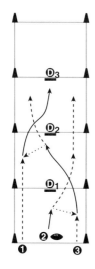

Explanation

Players commence as in the diagram.

Player 2 carries the ball towards Defender 1 who advances as soon as the attackers enter his grid.

Player 2 passes to one of his support players and he must immediately become alive as a support player.

The 3 attackers then advance down the corridor attempting to beat the advancing defenders who carry shields.

Ensure that the ball carrier understands he is always the vital decision maker.

Variations and Progressions

i) Condition the defenders' movement and/or decision making.

ii) Different number combinations, e.g., 3 v 2.

iii) Condition the ball carrier to bump off/hit and spin before off-loading.

3 v 2 Turn and Defend

Skills Developed

Passing and handling

Decision making

Support play

Communication

Level

Beginner/<u>Intermediate</u>/<u>Advanced</u>/All

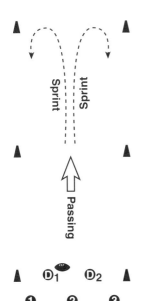

Explanation

D1 and D2 are defenders and start with a ball.

They jog interpassing to the first markers, place the ball on the ground, then sprint to the second markers before becoming live defenders.

A two-handed touch is used.

As soon as the ball is put on the ground, players 1, 2 and 3 sprint, pick it up and attack the two defenders in a 3 v 2 situation.

Variations and Progressions

i) Defenders placing the ball in the middle of the markers, then at either side gives different attacking problems to solve.

ii) 4 v 2 gives a further variation.

3 v 2 Turn

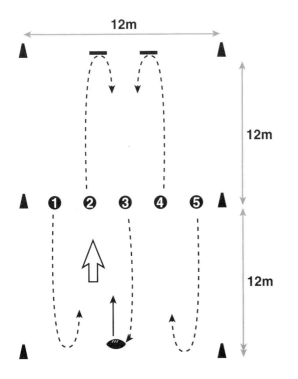

Skills Developed

Passing and handling

Decision making

Support play

Level

Beginner/Intermediate/<u>Advanced</u>/All

Explanation

Players begin as shown.

Coach calls two numbers out, e.g., 2 and 4.

Players 2 and 4 then sprint to the tackle shields and become 'live' defenders.

The other players sprint to the ball and become 'live' attackers.

This immediately leads to a 3 v 2 situation.

Variations and Progressions

i) Utilise groups of 3 and a 2 v 1 situation.

ii) Ball can be placed at one cone rather than in the middle so creating a different problem.

iii) Ball can be passed or rolled in by the coach.

(2 v 2) v 2

Skills Developed

Decision making

Passing and handling

Level

Beginner/Intermediate/Advanced/<u>All</u>

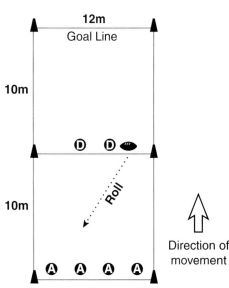

Explanation

The game is played along two grids.

Defenders start as shown and roll the ball to the attackers.

Attackers then attempt to score.

Attackers are allowed unlimited tackles, a tackle being a two-handed touch.

After a touch the ball is brought back into play with a pass.

Defenders must retire 5m after a touch.

Score as many tries in a certain time limit as possible.

Ensure that you rotate the defenders.

Variations and Progressions

i) Introduce a play-the-ball and each time a touch is made the defender must retire to their goal-line before becoming live defenders again. This encourages quick play-the-balls.

ii) Different number, e.g., 4 v 1, 3 v 1, 3 v 2 etc.

3 v 2 Two Sided Attack

Skills Developed   Passing and handling

Decision making

Communication

Support play

Level   Beginner/Intermediate/<u>Advanced</u>/All

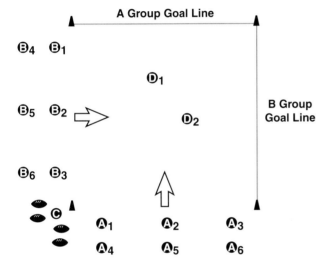

A Group Goal Line

B_4 B_1

D_1

B_5 B_2 D_2

B Group Goal Line

B_6 B_3

C A_1 A_2 A_3

A_4 A_5 A_6

Explanation

Players commence as shown 'A' Attackers in two groups of three. 'B' Attackers in two groups of three.

The coach (C) has balls readily available, as soon as he hands a ball to a group of 3 attackers, they attack the appropriate goal-line in a 3 v 2 situation.

The defenders are obviously at a disadvantage as they do not know from which direction the attack is coming from.

Defenders attempt to stop the attack with a two-handed touch or forcing an error.

The drill is continuous

3 v 2 Waves

Skills Developed   Passing and handling

Decision making

Timing of run

Level   Beginner/Intermediate/<u>Advanced</u>/All

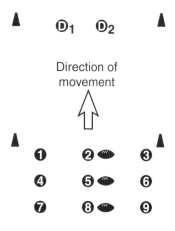

Direction of movement

Explanation

Attackers (Players 1 to 9) begin as shown in groups of three, middle attacker with the ball.

Two defenders (D1 and D2) start at the opposite end of the grid and can advance as soon as the first attacking group of 3 has entered the grid.

Defenders use a two-handed touch.

The 3 attackers use any means to outwit the two defenders.

The situation becomes very intense and game related by adding the following condition: after the three attackers have attempted to score, the two attackers who are not in possession of the ball become defenders.

The two previous defenders simply jog through with the ball carrier to the back of the attacking groups to become another wave of 3 attackers.

The drill is continuous.

Variations and Progressions

i) 2 v 1 for a lesser-ability group.

ii) Ball carrier starts at the end.

THE LONG PASS

The long pass gives width to an attack and asks questions of a defence, particularly when players who are receiving the ball run at different angles.

What to look for (Coaching Points)

The same as for the orthodox pass with the following exceptions:

1. The arms are taken further back.

2. The follow through is more pronounced as is the flick of the wrists.

3. The upper body should turn so that the shoulders are square and facing the receiver.

Note the follow through of the arms and eye on the target area as demonstrated by Henry Paul of Wigan and New Zealand.

THE SPIN PASS

The long pass is often accentuated in efficiency by spinning the ball. The spin pass propels the ball quickly a long way. When used widely it can give great width to the attack causing the opposition either to be outflanked or to spread, thereby creating gaps between players. It is an advanced skill which should not be introduced to players unless they have thoroughly mastered the other handling skills. Some young players become dependent upon the spin pass, losing the ability to weight a pass correctly.

It is very important to coach players to spin pass both to the left and to the right.

What to look for (Coaching Points)

1. Hold the ball as in the photograph.

2. The rear hand becomes dominant and propels the ball by moving forward and over it.

Other coaching points are as for the long pass.

Frano Botica, the former Wigan and Castleford stand off, demonstrates the classic hand positioning for the spin pass.

Cone Channels

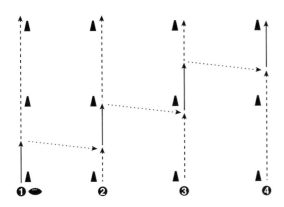

Skills Developed
Long passing

Level
Beginner/<u>Intermediate</u>/Advanced/All

Explanation
The practice area is arranged as shown.

The cones are positioned wide enough apart so as to encourage long passing.

Moving the Ball Wide – In Stages

Skills Developed   Organisation

Passing and handling

Level   Beginner/<u>Intermediate</u>/<u>Advanced</u>/All

Explanation

In groups of 6, 7 or 8.

Group move downfield passing the ball, emphasising width.

End man plays the ball, wide passing to the end of the line, the end man sprints for 15m, falls to the ground, regains his feet and plays the ball. The ball is then moved in the opposite direction to the end man. The drill continues as the group progress downfield.

Introduce the group to specific positions. Designate one player to be acting half-back, and have the same two players alternate between first and second receiver. The others in the group, the end man apart who is playing the ball, always take up wide positions whichever way the ball is being passed.

Emphasise, to the first and second receivers, moving the ball quickly wide without carrying it towards the opposition. The runners should straighten the line and take the ball at speed.

Markers are introduced to simulate the defence. One is placed where the ball is to be played and others are placed as a defensive line. The ball carriers cannot carry the ball through the cones, their objective is to move the ball outside the cones to a player running hard and straight. The group interpasses at speed down the field, attacking sets of cones appropriately spaced so as to practise wide passing to the left and to the right.

Increase the pressure by placing the cones in an arc so that they represent a defence which is moving up quickly. The ball carriers must again move the ball wide, round the outside cone to a runner.

The cones can now be replaced by defenders using tackle shields. The ball carriers again have to attempt to get on the outside of the defence with quick, wide passing.

Level 3

Timed Support

Skills Developed

Quick play-the-ball

Passing from the ground

Support play

Moving the ball wide

Level

Beginner/Intermediate/Advanced/All

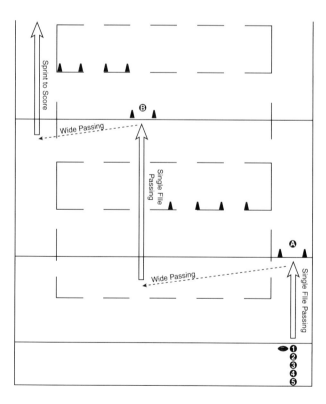

Explanation

Commence with the players as shown in the diagram. Then single file passing to point A, every player must handle the ball.

The player reaching point A falls, quickly regains his feet and plays the ball.

The ball is then passed quickly wide of the first line of cones. Again all players handle.

Immediately when wide of the cones, players revert to single-file passing. All players handle the ball before point B.

Player reaching point B falls, quickly regains his feet and plays the ball. The ball is then passed quickly wide of the next line of cones with all players handling before the end man bursts on to the ball and scores.

Split the players into equal groups and time the runs.

Time penalties should be given for errors or players not handling.

The winning group is the one with the quickest time.

Variations and Progressions

i) Passing wide left then wide right.

ii) Different skills incorporated.

Play-the-Ball Attack

Skills Developed

Quick play-the-ball

Fast passing and Handling

Support play

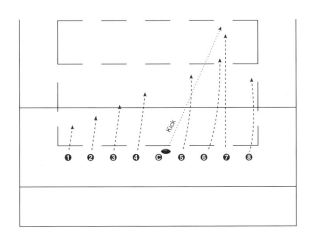

Level
Beginner/Intermediate/Advanced/<u>All</u>

Explanation

Coach with ball plus a line of players starts on the goal-line and jog forward. At some point the coach kicks the ball. One player retrieves the ball and plays it, another goes to acting half back and the rest form an attacking line. The ball is then quickly moved to the end player.

NB Use your discretion as to the size of the group.

Variations and Progressions

i) Angled runs and passing movements, e.g., runarounds can be introduced.

ii) Sets of plays can be introduced.

iii) At an advanced stage, defenders can be used to pressure the ball handlers.

Spin Pass Stages

Skills Developed   Spin pass

Level   <u>Beginner</u>/<u>Intermediate</u>/Advanced/All

Explanation

Pairs facing each other, gradually moving further apart.

Pairs move forward and pass sideways. Ensure player learns to pass both ways.

Game:

In groups of 4 attempt to pass the ball as far as possible between the players, using a static spin pass. Where the ball goes to ground, that is the distance achieved.

McHugh's Fast Hands Game

Skills Developed   Passing and handling

Offensive organisation and communication

Level   Beginner/<u>Intermediate</u>/Advanced/All

Explanation

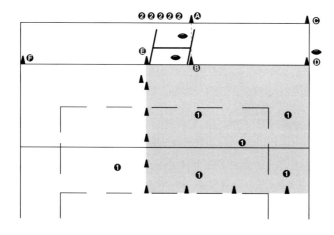

A player from Team 2 kicks a ball from between the posts into the shaded fielding area. The ball must bounce in this area or that player is 'out'.

The player must then pick up a ball on line AB, run and score a try at CD, pick up a ball at CD, sprint and score a try at AB. Team 1 must retrieve the ball, pass it according to the rules so that all of Team 1 handles the ball to score a try between EF.

If the player from Team 2 scores his try at AB before Team 1 score, he scores one point and kicks again. If Team 1 score a try between EF, the kicker is 'out' and replaced by another team member.

Additionally if the kick is caught on the full by a player from Team 1, the kicker is 'out'.

Team 1 become the kickers when all of Team 2 are 'out'.

Scores of each innings are kept.

Variations and Progressions

i) Fielding area is enlarged or made smaller.

ii) Type of kick is specified.

iii) Distance to be run can be amended.

THE SHORT PASS

The short pass is given to a support player who is moving close and usually at speed.

It is imperative that the ball is weighted properly so that it is easily caught.

That is the key coaching point.

What to look for (Coaching Points)

1. The ball should be held close to the body with arms bent and elbows in.
2. The ball should be guided with an upward flick of the wrists. The arms do not follow through.
3. The player should read the situation. At times the ball carrier can hand the ball to the receiver; at others the ball has to be flicked into the air enabling the support player to run on to it.

Single File Passing

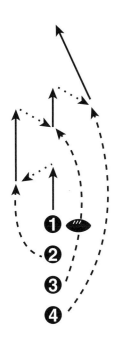

Skills Developed

Short pass

Weighting of the pass

Level

Beginner/<u>Intermediate</u>/Advanced/All

Explanation

The group move forward in single file with the ball carrier at the front.

The next player in line sprints through close to the ball carrier, who gives a short pass and then re-adjusts and re-joins the group at the back.

The drill continues as such.

Variations and Progressions

i) Passing in one direction only, i.e., continuous looping of players.

ii) Players support at random rather than in numerical order.

Level 3

THE QUICK PASS (fast hands)

An essential skill is to be able to pass in the shortest time possible. Advantages are as follows: when moving the ball across the field a quick passing action enables the runner to receive the ball before the defence moves up while a quick passing action often enables a player under pressure to make a successful pass prior to the tackle. Players making quick passes should catch and pass in one movement.

What to look for (Coaching Points)

A. When moving the ball across the field:

1. Reach out the hands to catch the ball early and immediately swing the arms in front of the body and release the ball in one movement.

2. When running at speed and passing to the right try to catch the ball as the right foot touches the ground and complete the pass before the left foot connects.

3. When passing to a receiver who is to make a quick pass the target is in front of his hands.

B. When passing under pressure:

1. Catch the ball close to the body and then release it with a quick flick of the wrists, concentrating both on the position of the support players and being aware of the position of the opposition.

2. Do not pass if there is doubt concerning:

a) the position of the receiver

b) the angle of the receiver's run

c) a possible interception

or

d) the receiver being tackled immediately he receives the ball.

Fast Hands

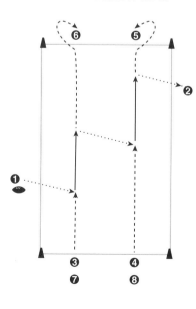

Skills Developed

Quick passing and handling

Level

Beginner/Intermediate/Advanced/<u>All</u>

Explanation

Players commence as shown.

Player 1 starts with the ball and passes to the advancing Player 3. Player 3 then gives a quick pass to 4 and 4 passes to 2.

2 then passes to the advancing 5, 5 to 6, 6 to 1.

1 then passes to the advancing 7, 7 to 8, 8 to 2.

The drill is continuous.

Players 1 and 2 remain simply as feeders.

Variations and Progressions

i) Move Players 1 and 2 nearer to each other so giving the passers less time.

ii) Increase number of line passers to 3.

iii) Have a corridor of feeders.

Shuttle Passing

Skills Developed   Quick hands

Line alignment

Concentration

Level   Beginner/Intermediate/Advanced/<u>All</u>

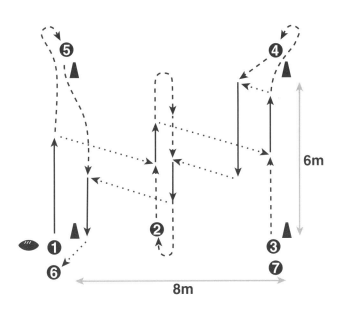

8m

6m

Explanation

Players start as in the diagram.

Player 1 runs with the ball, passes to 2 who passes to 3 who hands the ball to 4.

Players 1 and 3 remain at the top of the grid.

Then Player 4 begins progressing to the bottom of the grid before passing to 2 who in turn passes to 5, who hands on to 6.

The sequence then is: 6 pass to 2 pass to 7 hand on to 3, and the drill is continuous.

It is important to set the number of shuttle runs that the middle player (2) does before changing positions.

Variations and Progressions

i) Can be done with 7, 9, 11 or 13 players.

The more players the greater the rest periods.

Angled Quick Hands

Skills Developed	Passing and handling
	Communication
	Unit ability to 'stand up' a slide defence.
Level	Beginner/Intermediate/<u>Advanced</u>/All

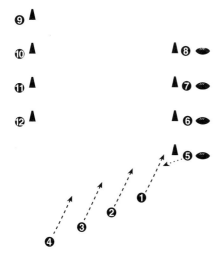

Explanation

Players line up as in diagram and run as indicated.

Player 5 passes to 1, 1 to 2, 2 to 3 and 3 to 4.

In the meantime player 5 has followed player 4 and passes to player 12, who remains on the cone.

Player 1 then remains on the cone previously occupied by Player 5.

Player 6 then serves to 2, on to 3, 3 to 4, 4 to 5, 5 to 6, then to Player 11. Player 2 then remains on the cone previously occupied by Player 6.

The drill then follows as such with all the runners angled towards the feeders.

THE LOOP ROUND

This is when one player passes to another, then runs around his back to receive a return pass. Again this is an important skill when attempting to break a line defence.

Initially the pivot should turn in such a way that the player on the move is always in his vision and the receiver can always see the ball.

An alternative is for a player to loop around while supporting a player running with the ball. This is most effective if the ball carrier faces forward all the time, relying on peripheral vision and communication.

The line should move down field and not across. The receiver must, therefore, run across field in an arc to get into position then straighten up before receiving the pass.

What to look for (Coaching Points)

1. Immediately after passing, follow the ball.
2. Loop round but come on to the ball running straight and attacking the goal-line.

In vision

3. The ball carrier turns towards the runner keeping him in sight while the runner can see the ball.
4. The pass may be made early, the ball carrier executing the pass at speed, by merely turning his upper body from the waist. Otherwise he must execute a full turn and will be almost stationary when the pass is executed.

Out of vision

5. The pass is made late when the player on the loop has passed completely round the back of the ball carrier.
6. Communication is important, with the player on the loop conveying his intentions to the ball carrier.
7. The support player needs to arc sharply, arriving close beside the ball carrier.
8. There is more chance of creating a gap for the receiver to run through, if the passer drifts away from the direction of the pass and tries to pull the defence with him.
9. The pass should not be made blind: the ball carrier should see the support player before the pass is made (this is normally out the corner of the eye, i.e., peripheral vision).
10. The movement should be executed at speed.

Individual Loop

Level 3

Skills Developed   Passing and handling

Level   Beginner/<u>Intermediate</u>/<u>Advanced</u>/All

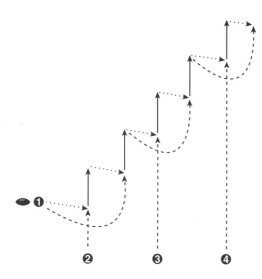

Explanation

Players commence as shown.

Player 1 passes to 2 who advances the ball, 1 loops around 2 and receives the ball back.

1 then passes to 3 who advances the ball, 1 loops around 3 and receives the ball back.

The drill continues.

NB Encourage straight running in order for it to be effective.

Variations and Progressions

i) As above but Player 1, rather than looping every player, simply loops to the end of the line.

ii) As in variation (i) except after Player 1 loops to the end of the line, so do 2, 3 and 4 after him.

THE DROP OFF

An excellent handling ploy which serves to change the angle of the attack.

What to look for (Coaching Points)

1. The ball carrier runs diagonally towards the outside.

2. The ball carrier has his support in vision on the outside.

3. The pass is made as the two players cross.

4. The ball carrier executes the pass turning outwards so that the support player is always in vision and the support player can always see the ball. The pass is a gentle inside pass into the bread basket executed with the wrists and fingertips – weighting of the pass is essential.

5. Timing of ball carrier and support player is essential.

It is possible to carry out this skill with a two-handed or one-handed pass. A one-handed pass is normally for more advanced players.

Corridor Drop Off

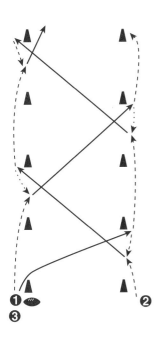

Skills Developed

Passing and handling

Timing of run

Angle of run

Level

Beginner/Intermediate/<u>Advanced</u>/All

Explanation

One ball to each group of 3 players. A row of markers set out as shown. Player 1 starts with the ball and angles diagonally to drop off 2 at the marker, 2 then drops off 3 at the next marker, 3 drops off 1, and so on.

It is important to stress that only the ball carrier runs diagonally across the corridor. Support runners should always run straight along the outside of the corridor until they drop off and receive the ball.

NB Corridor can extend for as long as you desire. Many groups of 3 can be catered for if you stagger the start of each group.

The drop-off pass. For beginners, the two-handed version ensures better ball control although Jonathan Davies shows the more advanced skill.

Partner Drop off

Skills Developed

Passing and handling

Timing of run

Angle of run

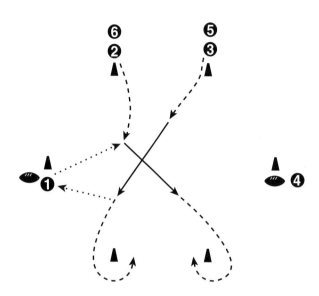

Level

Beginner/<u>Intermediate</u>/Advanced/All

Explanation

Players start the drill as shown in the diagram.

Player 1 stationary as a feeder throughout. He passes the ball to Player 2 who has advanced from his starting cone. 2 then cuts across to drop off. Player 3 on an angled run. 3 receives the ball and passes the ball back to Player 1. Both 2 and 3 continue running to the end cones.

On completion of this pattern, Player 4 who is stationary as a feeder passes to 5, 5 angles across and drops off 6, 6 passes back to Player 4, 5 and 6 run to end cones.

The drill continues with these alternate drop off patterns from the two feeders.

PLAY-THE-BALL

The background to the play-the-ball and the coaching points, i.e., what to look for in the play-the-ball are included in this section as it would be remiss to omit them from here when we are also looking at passing the ball from the ground.

The play-the-ball movement restarts play after a tackle. A quick, efficient play-the-ball enables the team in possession to launch sustained attacks.

On average, there are more than 300 play-the-ball movements in a game of Rugby League so it is a vital technique to learn.

Players must realise that a ball which is brought slowly back into play allows the defence time to retreat the required distance and to re-group. A fast play-the-ball is likely to catch the defence out of position and moving backwards. Obviously, an unprepared defence is far easier to attack so the importance of the following cannot be over emphasised.

A player must regain his feet quickly, play the ball smoothly, and the dummy half must give a technically efficient pass from the ground.

Explanation

The tackled player having retained possession regains his feet as quickly as possible bringing the ball up with him.

Facing the opponents' goal-line, he places the ball alongside his foremost foot.

After the ball has touched the ground, the player plays the ball back as smoothly as possible giving the acting half-back every chance of passing quickly from the ground.

What to look for (Coaching Points)

1. The tackled player should regain his feet as quickly as possible facing the opponents' goal-line and lifting the ball clear of the ground.

2. Whilst regaining his feet he should secure the ball.

3. Whilst bending the body well forward, he places the ball in front of and by the inside of his front foot longways on and releases it.

4. Simultaneously, he places the sole of his other foot on top of the ball.

5. He rolls the ball back with full control.

6. The acting half-back should pass from the ground.

In photograph 1 our young player places the ball alongside his foremost foot, and photograph 2 shows the correct foot positioning for ball control.

PASSING FROM THE GROUND

This is a skill similar to the pass from the waist, but the ball should be passed directly from the ground. It is used in most play-the-ball movements and also from the base of the scrum. Unless the acting half-back is going to run with the ball, he should not pick it up as this wastes time and allows the defence to advance. Thus passing from the ground is the springboard of many attacks and correct technique is essential. Particular care is needed to ensure that each pass is correctly weighted and executed in the shortest possible time.

What to look for (Coaching Points)

1. Be aware of the speed of the receiver, the position of the target and the weight of the pass required.

2. Bend over the ball.

3. Hold the ball firmly in both hands and be prepared to pass from the ground.

4. Turn the head and upper body towards the target.

5. Pass from the ground without lifting the ball up and without straightening the back.

6. As the pass is made the nearest foot will be in front of the body pointing at the receiver.

7. The ball is aimed to the bread basket in front of the receiver. The distance in front depends on the speed of the receiver.

8. The ball is directed by the fingers and wrists.

9. There is a follow through with the arms so that finally they are fully extended towards the receiver with fingers pointing at the target.

Basic Pairs Play-the-Ball

Skills Developed   Play-the-ball

Level   Beginner/Intermediate/Advanced/All

Explanation

Players commence as in diagram.

Player 1 with the ball falls to the ground, then regains his feet as quickly as possible, bringing the ball up with him. He then places the ball alongside his foremost foot longways on, simultaneously he places his other foot on top of the ball and the ball is rolled back with full control.

Player 2 then picks the ball up, turns around completely, drops to the floor and repeats the process as described, playing the ball to player 1.

The drill is continuous.

*Keiron Cunningham of St. Helens and
Wales demonstrates excellent technique
when passing from the ground.*

Continuous play-the-ball

Skills Developed   Gathering a rolling ball

Quick play-the-ball

Level   <u>Beginner</u>/Intermediate/Advanced/All

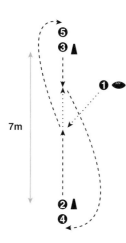

7m

Explanation

Player I starts with the ball as shown in the diagram and rolls it towards player 2.

Player 2 advances, dives on the ball, regains his feet and plays it. Player I has run immediately upon rolling the ball to dummy half. Player 2 then joins the opposite line behind player 5.

Meanwhile player I rolls the ball towards player 3. Player 3 advances, dives on the ball and plays it. Player I runs to dummy half, picks up and rolls to player 4. The drill continues with Player I acting as dummy half. After a set period of time, another player adopts the dummy half feeder role.

Variations and Progressions

i) After the ball has been rolled, the player who has last played the ball pressurises the receiver of the rolled ball.

Level 2

Off-the-Floor Passing

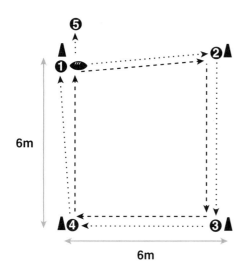

6m

6m

Skills Developed

Passing and handling

Level

<u>Beginner</u>/Intermediate/Advanced/All

Explanation

Players commence as in the diagram.

Player I passes the ball off the floor to Player 2. He upon receiving the ball places it on the floor.

Meanwhile, Player I has followed his own pass to 2 and passes it off the ground to 3 who receives the ball and places it on the ground.

Player I follows and passes to 4 and the drill continues as above until Player 2 receives once again.

He then becomes the off-the-ground passer and follower of the ball.

The drill continues until every player has passed and followed the ball around the grid.

Variations and Progressions

i) The player receiving the ball immediately goes to the ground, regains his feet and plays the ball.

Basic Sixes Play-the-Ball

Skills Developed   Play the ball
Passing from the ground

Level   Beginner/Intermediate/Advanced/All

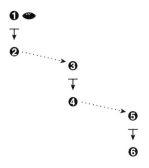

Explanation

Players commence as in diagram.

Player I starts with the ball on the ground. On command, he regains his feet and quickly plays the ball to 2.

2 passes from the ground to 3 who receives, falls to the ground, regains his feet and plays the ball properly to 4.

4 passes to 5, who plays the ball to 6.

When 6 receives the ball, all players about turn and the ball is worked back along the line in the same way until I receives it.

Variations and Progressions

i) Competition between groups.

Fours Play-the-Ball

Skills Developed

Play-the-ball

Passing from the ground

Level

Beginner/Intermediate/Advanced/All

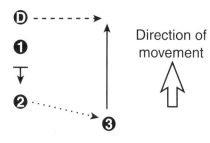

Direction of movement

Explanation

Player 1 plays the ball to 2, 2 is the acting half-back, 3 is the first receiver and D the marker.

The defender (D) should put pressure on the ball carrier who ensures that the ball is played quickly and correctly.

The acting half-back should pass from the ground.

The receiver should receive the ball going forward.

The defender should halt progress via a two-handed touch or grab.

Variations and Progressions

i) Increase the intensity of the opposition gradually.

Dummy Half Link Up

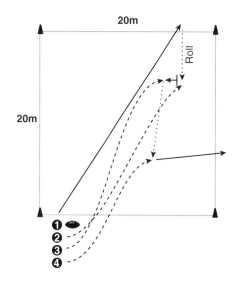

20m

20m

Roll

Skills Developed

Playing the ball at speed

Dummy half passing

Timing of run

Level

Beginner/Intermediate/Advanced/All

Explanation

Player 1 starts with the ball and runs across any of the grid boundaries (goal-lines) and scores a try. He then rolls the ball into the grid in any direction at which time the other players set off. Player 2 retrieves the ball and plays it facing the nearest grid boundary. Player 3 goes to dummy-half and passes to player 4 who scores a try.

Player 4 then rolls the ball, 1 plays the ball, 2 goes to dummy half and passes, 3 scores and rolls the ball into the grid. The drill then continues.

NB The drill can be made competitive by giving the players a set time to work within.

Variations and Progressions

i) Introduce 2 teams of 4 working in the same area.

Evasion and the Offensive Collision

A player who is elusive, has tremendous foot coordination and is difficult to tackle is not only a crowd pleaser, but also an important weapon in the attacking armoury of the team. Such players who can beat defenders in a one-on-one situation are developed via working on various methods of evasion and breaking a tackle. Coaches should devote time to developing these important skills in order to create a rounded player.

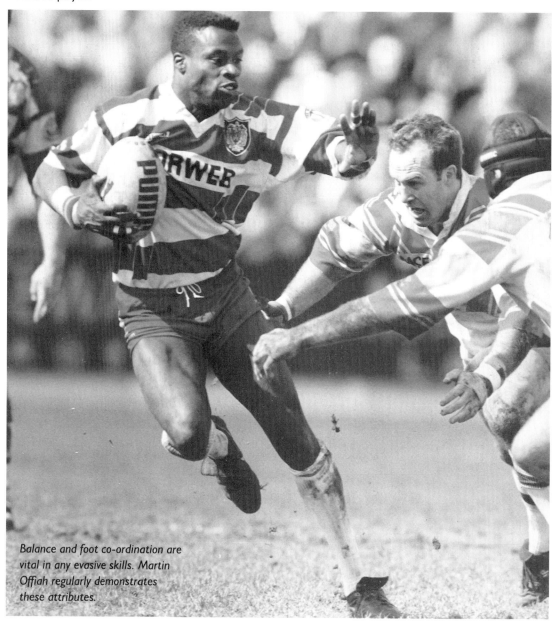

Balance and foot co-ordination are vital in any evasive skills. Martin Offiah regularly demonstrates these attributes.

1. Side Step

The side step is a sudden, quick change of direction followed by an immediate straightening up.

What to look for (Coaching Points)

a) The player should run at the defender at speed.

b) When 2–5m from the defender, drive the toes of either foot powerfully into the ground and thrust off in the other direction.

c) Accelerate into the gap and straighten up.

d) The skill should be performed without shortening stride and at maximum speed.

Francis Cummins sizes up a would-be defender for a side step off his right foot.

2. Change of Pace

The change of pace is sudden acceleration of the ball carrier causing the would-be tackler to mistime his tackle.

What to look for (Coaching Points)

a) The player should be aware of the speed and direction of the would-be tackler.

b) Slow down slightly forcing the would-be tackler to alter his position and timing.

c) Suddenly accelerate sharply away.

3. Swerve

This technique takes the ball carrier in a wide arc around his opponents or around the cover defence. It should be executed at maximum speed.

What to look for (Coaching Points)

a) The player should change direction around the would-be tackler.

b) The change of direction is sudden but not as extreme as the side step.

c) The path of the ball carrier is an arc away from the defender.

d) The hips should also sway away from the tackler.

e) Balance is vital.

4. Dummy Pass

The ball carrier makes a passing motion but retains possession of the ball, thus encouraging the defence to switch its attention from the ball carrier to the support player.

What to look for (Coaching Points)

a) The player should look at the would-be receiver.

b) Take the arms back and make as if to execute a pass, perhaps even exaggerate the motion.

c) Follow through with the arms.

d) Retain possession.

5. Breaking the Tackle

There are few skills more satisfying than breaking through the opposition's defence. To do so requires the combination of technique, determination and self-confidence.

What to look for (Coaching Points)

a) The player should run with determination.

b) Hold the ball firmly.

c) Accelerate at the gap.

d) Brace the body.

e) Hit the would-be tackler with the chest or shoulders.

f) Have one foot on the ground at the point of impact.

6. The Bump Off

It is important for all players to practise contact skills.

Such practices not only encourage the player to break tackles, but develop sufficient self-confidence to run into the collision with determination.

The ball carrier should use the hard part of his body, particularly the shoulder or hip to bump off the opponent. When using the chest the player should be encouraged to fold his arms over the ball, hands upwards and elbows downwards, and take the brunt of the collision on the forearm.

What to look for (Coaching points)

   a) The player should size up the would-be tackler.

   b) Run with determination.

   c) At the correct moment thrust the shoulders, hip or chest with full power into the would-be tackler.

   d) Drive the legs ensuring that one foot is in contact with the ground at the moment of impact.

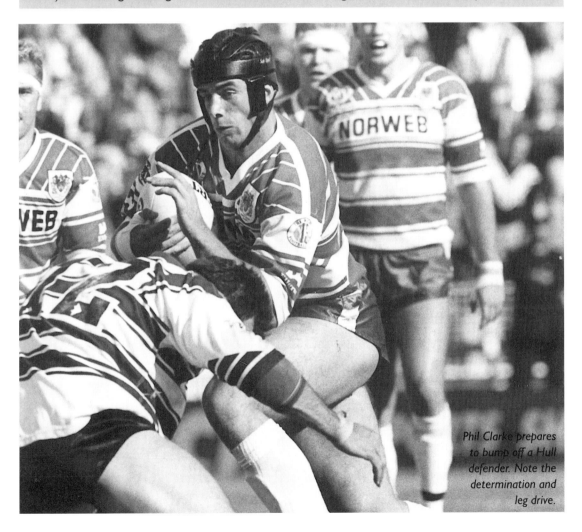

Phil Clarke prepares to bump off a Hull defender. Note the determination and leg drive.

7. Hit and Spin

The hit and spin is an evasive tactic which originated in American football. At the point of impact the ball carrier spins off the defender and either off-loads the ball or makes ground.

A further recent development by players such as Henry Paul at Wigan, has been to spin prior to collision.

Both of these techniques need to be implemented.

Collision hit and spin – what to look for (Coaching Points)

    a) Hold the ball firmly.

    b) Take short steps.

    c) Pump the legs quickly through the entire operation.

    d) When moving to the right, hit with the right shoulder and spin turning to the left with the back into the tackle, keeping the ball available.

    e) Dip the shoulder on the point of impact. If spinning to the left (d) should be reversed.

Spin prior to the collision – what to look for (Coaching Points)

    a) Hold the ball firmly.

    b) Take short steps.

    c) Pump the legs quickly throughout the entire spin.

    d) When moving to the right, dip the right shoulder and spin, turning to the left with the back to the tackler, keeping the ball available and also being aware if a gap opens up to accelerate into and through it.

8. Hand Off or Fend

The hand off is a forceful thrust of the arm, open palm outwards, into the head, chest or shoulder of the would-be tackler. The ball carrier either forcefully pushes the tackler away or uses the tackler's own momentum to push himself out of the way.

Inexperienced players should be made to realise that the hand off is a thrusting motion and should not be encouraged to run with an arm out.

Timing is vital.

What to look for (Coaching Points)

    a) Size up the would-be tackler.

    b) At the correct moment the ball carrier thrusts his arm open palm outwards into the head, chest or shoulder of the would-be tackler.

    c) The arm should be bent when contact is made and then immediately straightened.

    d) As the arm is straightened the ball carrier should push on the opponent to take him away from the tackler.

Combination practices should be designed to encourage players to select the methods of evasion and breaking a tackle which are best suited to a particular situation.

Steve Prescott of St. Helens straightens the arm from a hand off which pushes him away from Wigan's Terry O'Connor

THE PASS IN THE COLLISION

The ability to pass the ball whilst being tackled is a most valuable skill to develop. It falls into two major categories (a) driving through the tackle and passing, or (b) turning in the tackle and passing.

a) Driving through the tackle and passing

The ball carrier drives with determination into the tackler, holds the ball firmly and passes around the back of the tackler. The advantage of this is that despite the ball carrier being tackled, the ball is passed to a support player who has already penetrated the defensive line.

What to look for (Coaching Points)

1. Hold the ball firmly, preferably in two hands.

2. Drive with determination into the tackle, lifting the body up and forward.

3. Thrust the ball forward behind the tackler and be prepared to make a quick, accurate pass to the support player.

4. Make a visual check and pass only to an unmarked player.

5. If support is not immediately available, bring the ball into the chest in order to control possession.

Brian McDermott of Bradford Bulls thrusts the ball beyond the tackler and looks before passing to a support player.

(Picture by Sig Kasatkin)

b) Turning in the tackle and passing

The ball carrier attempts to break the tackle, but if unsuccessful, he turns in the tackle to face his own in-goal area and makes the ball available. This can be done after the player has attempted to bump off the opponent or spins out of the tackle of the opponent.

What to look for (Coaching Points)

1. Hold the ball firmly.
2. Drive with determination into the tackle and attempt to break through.
3. If unsuccessful turns toward the in goal area putting the body between the tackler and the ball.
4. Pass if an unmarked player is available.

Denis Betts turns in the tackle and off-loads with his body between the tackler and the ball.

With the pass in the collision, decision making should be introduced.

As the ball carrier either thrusts his body through into space or hits the collision and looks to off-load, he should make a conscious decision whether a successful pass will be made. If so, he should continue with his actions; if not, he should secure possession and make the ball safe.

Side Step Run

Level 2

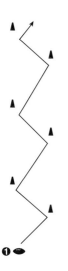

Skills Developed

Side step

Level

<u>Beginner</u>/Intermediate/Advanced/All

Explanation

Player with the ball side steps the markers.

Variations and Progressions

i) Passive opposition instead of the marker.

Change of Pace Run

Level 2

Skills Developed   Change of pace

Level   <u>Beginner</u>/Intermediate/Advanced/All

Explanation

In pairs, one player carries the ball, the other shadows, in a restricted area for control.

On the coach's command the ball carrier accelerates, and the shadow has to respond and stay within arm's length. When the coach instructs slow and the player decelerates, the shadow again has to respond.

The drill continues as such.

Variations and Progressions

i) Use markers to signal acceleration and deceleration zones.

ii) Have the ball carrier accelerate/decelerate of his own accord which makes it more difficult for the shadow.

In and Out

Skills Developed

The body swerve

Level

<u>Beginner</u>/Intermediate/Advanced/All

Explanation

Players carrying the ball swerve in alternate directions.

Variations and Progressions

i) Passive opposition instead of the marker.

Dummy ball

Skills Developed   Dummy pass

Level   <u>Beginner</u>/Intermediate/Advanced/All

Explanation

Player carrying the ball runs at a marker and throws a dummy pass to the left, progresses, throws one to the right and so on.

Variations and Progressions

i) Passive opposition instead of the marker.

Level 3

Breaking the Tackle

Skills Developed   Running through the collision

Level   Beginner/Intermediate/Advanced/<u>All</u>

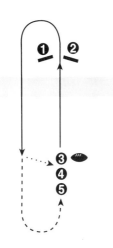

Explanation

Players 1 and 2 with shields.

Player 3 starts with the ball and runs with correct technique and determination through the shield barrier before turning and passing to Player 4 who repeats the drill.

Variations and Progressions

i) Condition the shield holders for varying degrees of resistance.

ii) As above except that after breaking the shield barrier the ball carrier should feed the pass to the next runner just prior to impact (the shaded area in the diagram). This would put more pressure on the receiver.

Level 3

Hit and Spin Series

Skills Developed   Hit and Spin

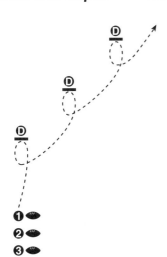

Level
Beginner/Intermediate/Advanced/<u>All</u>

Explanation
The ball carriers hit the defenders, who are holding shields, with their right shoulders turning to the left and spinning towards the right and into the next shield.

It is important for players to develop a spin to both right and left.

Variations and Progressions
i) With amended shield positions, the same drill can be used for the bump off.

ii) Individual work can be done in a small area, e.g., Player 1 rebounding off the defenders, who are holding shields, practising hitting, and reversing direction to hit another defender.

Hand Off Gauntlet

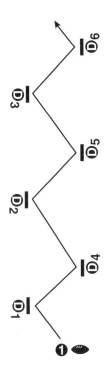

Skills Developed

Hand off

Ball carrying technique

Level

<u>Beginner</u>/Intermediate/Advanced/All

Explanation

Players in single file with a ball each.

The players run the gauntlet handing off each defender who is holding a shield.

Defenders (D1 to D6) should be knelt holding a tackle shield at chest height facing into the corridor.

Encourage the ball carrier to switch the hands carrying the ball as he approaches the defender.

Variations and Progressions

i) As competence improves incorporate a side step with the hand off.

ii) Passive opposition can be used.

Body Through and Pass

Skills Developed

Passing in the tackle

Level

Beginner/Intermediate/Advanced/<u>All</u>

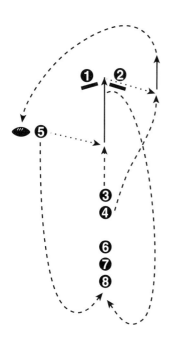

Explanation

Players 1 and 2 with shields.

Player 5 passes the ball to 3, 3 runs between the shields and thrusts his upper body upwards and forwards through the shields, passing to Player 4 in close support.

NB It is essential that the shields are held lower than usual, at lower chest height with the two holders standing close together.

Player 4 then becomes the feeder and the player who has hit the shields and passed in the tackle goes to the back of the line as does Player 5.

Variations and Progressions

i) To introduce the technique it could be practised unopposed or with passive defenders.

ii) The same drills can be used for turning in the tackle and passing where a player is unable to break the shield defence. In this both a one-handed and two-handed pass should be practised.

iii) Continuous banks of shields can be used.

Cone Evasion

Skills Developed

Foot coordination for evasive skills
Ball carrying techniques

Level

<u>Beginner</u>/<u>Intermediate</u>/Advanced/All

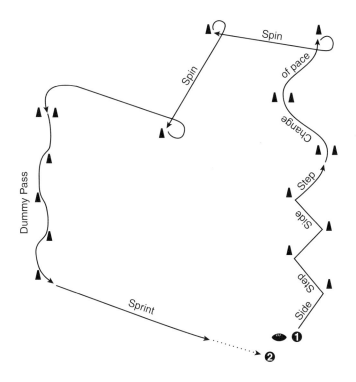

Explanation

Player 1 starts with the ball – markers are arranged as shown.

Player 1 side steps off alternate feet before going through two gates with a change of pace at each.

He then does a 'Henry Paul' spin at the next three markers before going through the gate to throw dummy passes to alternate sides before sprinting and passing the ball to Player 2.

The drill continues.

To introduce competition individuals may be timed or teams could run as a relay.

Variations and Progressions

i) Different combinations.

ii) Incorporate shields.

iii) Incorporate contact evasive skills.

iv) Incorporate support.

Evasion Grid

Skills Developed

Different methods of evasion

Level

Beginner/Intermediate/Advanced/All

Explanation

In a ten metre square grid one defender has to tackle as many of the four ball carriers as possible in thirty seconds.

The four ball carriers can use any method of evasion to stay 'alive' for the allotted time.

Level 3

Bust and Pass

Skills Developed   Receiving a pass under pressure

Determined running

Passing under pressure

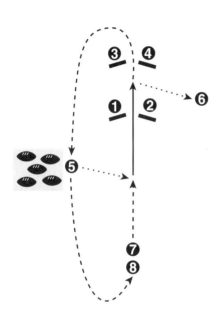

Level

Beginner/Intermediate/Advanced/<u>All</u>

Explanation

Several balls are stored in the shaded area.

Player 7 advances towards the shields, receives a pass from 5, bursts through the first bank of shields (held by Players 1 and 2) before passing to Player 6 prior to contact with the second set of shields (held by Players 3 and 4).

7 then replaces 5 as feeder and 5 line up behind Player 8.

Variations and Progressions

i) Condition the resistance of the shield holders.

ii) Can be run as a corridor of shields.

iii) Support players can be introduced.

Level 3

3 v 2 Shields

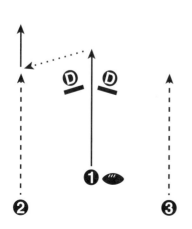

Skills Developed   Determined running

Close support play

Decision making

Level

Beginner/<u>Intermediate</u>/<u>Advanced</u>/All

Explanation

Player 1 starts with the ball and runs hard through the defenders holding the shields. Players 2 and 3 are in support. 1 passes to either 2 or 3.

Variations and Progressions

i) Player 1 receives the ball just prior to contact with the shields.

ii) A corridor of shields is faced by the 3 attackers at regular intervals.

iii) A fourth attacker is added who is positioned directly behind Player 1 (the ball carrier). The shields then try to prevent the ball carrier busting and he must turn and off-load to the fourth attacker who in turn must read the situation and time his run at the correct side of the collision.

iv) This can be developed into team play from a play-the-ball or other situations.

v) Can be incorporated into continuous or combination practices.

Hit, Spin, Off-load

Skills Developed   As in title
Support play

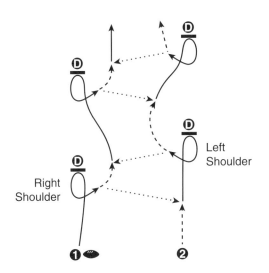

Right Shoulder

Left Shoulder

Level Beginner/Intermediate/Advanced/<u>All</u>

Explanation

A bank of shields is spaced appropriately.

Player 1 starts with the ball hits, spins and passes to the supporting Player 2.

2 repeats the process passing to Player 1 who has assumed the support role.

The drill is continuous.

Ensure fast, pumping feet and correct decision making.

Variations and Progressions

i) Can be used with appropriate adjustments for the bump off and turning in the tackle before off-loading.

See-Saw

Skills Developed

Support play

Hit, spin and off-load

Timing of run

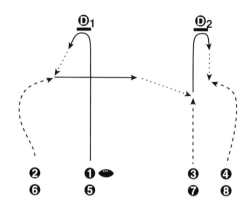

Level
Beginner/<u>Intermediate</u>/<u>Advanced</u>/All

Explanation

Player 1 runs with the ball, hits the shield, spins and off-loads to Player 2 who gives a flat pass to Player 3 who in turn hits, spins and off-loads to Player 4. Player 4 then gives a flat pass to Player 5 and the sequence continues. It is important that the shields retain their position.

After each involvement, the players return to the back of the line.

Variations and Progressions

i) More support players.

ii) Bump off rather than hit and spin.

iii) Bump off or the hit and spin.

iv) Instead of a flat pass, a drop off may be used which would mean the receiver runs diagonally to the shield rather than straight.

See-Saw Extension

Skills Developed

Support play

Hit, spin and off-load

Timing of run

Wide passing

Level

Beginner/Intermediate/<u>Advanced</u>/All

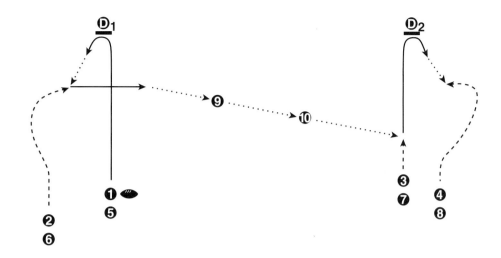

Explanation

Player 1 runs with the ball, hits the shield (held by D1) spins and off-loads to Player 2 who gives a flat pass to Player 9, whose job is to move the ball quickly and wide to the next wide passer (10). 10 then gives a wide pass to Player 3 who hits, spins and off-loads to player 4.

Player 4 then gives a flat pass to 10 who picks up 9, and he gives a wide pass to Player 5 and the sequence continues. It is important that the shields retain their position.

Ensure that 9 and 10 always re-position so that the passing is always backwards.

After each involvement, Players 1 to 8 return to the back of the lines.

Level 3

Pass and Follow Support

Skills Developed   Close support play

Decision making

Pass and Follow support

Determined running

Level   Beginner/<u>Intermediate</u>/<u>Advanced</u>/All

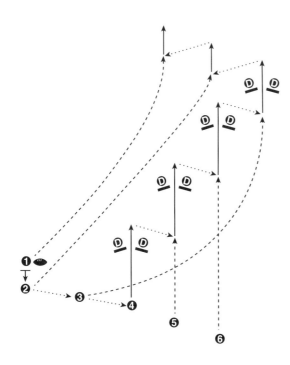

Explanation

Defenders line up as shown with a tackle shield.

Player 1 plays the ball to 2 who in turn passes to the first receiver, Player 3. 3 passes to 4 who hits the defensive line and busts before passing to 5 who busts and passes to 6 who busts and passes to Player 3.

3 has trailed the ball from his original first receiver position.

Players 1 and 2 who originally started at the play-the-ball support on the inside to score.

Encourage 4, 5 and 6 to support off Players 1 and 2.

Variations and Progressions

i) Different defender combinations.

ii) Different off-load situations, e.g., hit and spin, bump off, etc.

iii) Inside and outside support.

iv) Covering winger, full back situation incorporated.

Bust and Support

Skills Developed   Control of the ball

Evasive skills

Support play

Decision making

Off-load in the tackle

Passing and handling

Level   Beginner/<u>Intermediate</u>/<u>Advanced</u>/All

Explanation

A group of players commence with the ball attacking defenders 4, 5 and 6 who are all carrying shields.

The ball carrying group must penetrate the shields using close support play.

The moment they break in the clear, they are confronted by the match-like situation of full back (D1) and wingers/cover defenders (D2 and D3).

Variations and Progressions

i) Restrict the evasive skill in the first corridor to hit and spin, bump off, etc.

ii) Before embarking upon this final combination, it may be worth playing 5 v the full back, 5 v full back and winger, 5 v full back and two wingers.

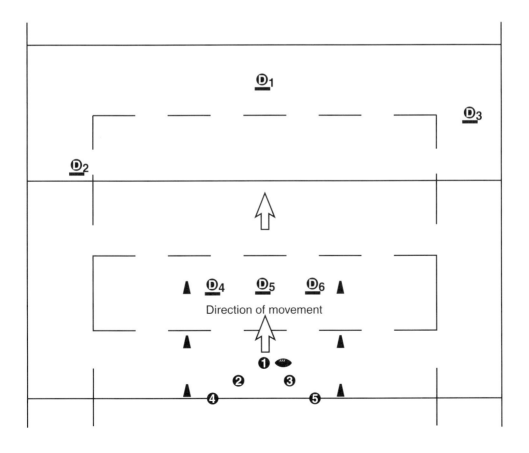

Bust and Finish

Skills Developed

Breaking the tackle

Decision making

Passing and handling

Level

Beginner/Intermediate/Advanced/All

Explanation

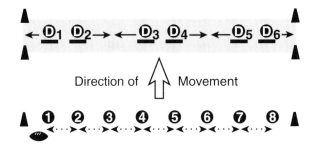

Players commence as shown.

Attackers (Players 1 to 8) are static line passing.

D1 and D2 work in pairs, D3 and D4 work in pairs, and D5 and D6 work in pairs.

These three defensive pairs can only move laterally within the shaded area.

D7 and D8 are individual wild card defenders.

The attackers interpass the ball until the coach blows a whistle.

Upon this the attacker in possession runs at and busts whichever gap is nearest, i.e., between D1 and D2, D3 and D4 or D5 and D6. The rest of the attackers follow quickly in support.

After the attackers bust through the gap and come out of the shaded area, D7 and D8 come into play as live defenders.

The attackers then continue to advance the ball over the goal-line.

Upon scoring, the attackers sprint back to the start position and immediately begin another attack.

Count how many tries are scored in 3 minutes, then change over.

Variations and Progressions

6 attackers and no wild card defenders.

The attackers would then attack one way and immediately turn to attack the other.

If this variation is played, the shaded area must be equidistant from each goal-line.

KICKING AND GAINING POSSESSION

Rugby League is essentially a handling game. However, kicking is a skill which also plays an important part in its scoring and tactics. All inexperienced players when learning the game should have the opportunity to become adept at the kicking skills, although as players play in a higher standard of competition and specialism becomes the norm, only the selected few would practise such skills.

1. The Punt

The punt is kicking the ball from the hand and is used to:

> a) Gain ground from a penalty kick: from a penalty kick the ball may be kicked directly out of play over the touchline without bouncing.
>
> b) Gain touch directly from play: in order to gain territory the ball must first of all bounce in the field of play before crossing the touchline.
>
> c) Take play down field: in this case the kicking team are content to give away possession in order to gain territorial advantage. It is important for the chasers to comply with the Laws of the Game before completing the tackle.

There are two forms of punt. The Torpedo is used when the aim is to gain a great deal of distance or height and the ball spins through the air. The Orthodox method is easier to execute and is used to kick accurately over a short distance.

The correct execution of both types of punt depends greatly upon:

> a) the way the ball is held
>
> b) the way the ball is guided to contact with the foot
>
> c) positioning of the foot at the point of contact
>
> d) the follow through.

Because the Orthodox punt is more easily executed, it should be introduced before the Torpedo.

Orthodox Punt – what to look for (Coaching Points)

a) Hold the ball as for passing. Since the kick is often used as a snap tactic in general play, it is an advantage not to change the position of the hands on the ball.

b) Line up with the target so that the shoulders are square.

c) The head should be down and the eyes kept on the ball until it has been kicked.

d) The ball should be held a comfortable distance away from the body and guided down to the point of contact with the foot.

e) The round of the ball should fit into the round of the boot.

f) The toes are straightened by being forced downwards from the ankle.

g) Drive through the ball and follow through towards the target.

NB For beginners, the ball may be held point to point to ensure initial success.

h) Head and eyes remain down.

The Orthodox Punt

The Torpedo Punt

The Torpedo Punt – what to look for (Coaching Points)

The coaching points are identical to those for the Orthodox punt except that:

a) The right hand should be placed slightly under and to the rear of the right-hand side of the ball and the left hand placed in a similar manner, underneath and to the front of the left-hand side (vice versa for left-footed kickers).

b) The ball should feel comfortable in the hands and should be pointing slightly inwards.

c) The kicking foot should be angled slightly inwards as it meets the ball. This imparts the spin which gives the Torpedo punt greater distance.

Jonathan Davies demonstrates excellent technique for the torpedo punt.

2. The Chip Kick

The aim of such a kick is to breach a well organised defence. In this case the ball is kicked over the heads of the opposition for the kicker or a team mate to chase and regather.

What to look for (Coaching Points)

The coaching points are identical to the Punt except that the foot is slightly cocked and does not follow through. The foot lifts the ball over a short distance. Correct weighting of the ball is exceptionally important and the kicker should be able to perform this skill both standing and in motion.

3. The Bomb

The Bomb, or up-and-under, is a punt which is directed high into the air. The intention of this tactical kick is to enable the kicking side to arrive underneath the ball from an on-side position thereby regaining possession or putting the catcher under extreme pressure.

What to look for (Coaching Points)

The coaching points are as for the Punt but:

a) The body leans backwards.
b) The foot makes contact directly under the ball.
c) The drive of the foot is upwards.
d) The point of contact of the ball with the foot is usually vertical to the Punt.

NB The inexperienced player may have success holding the ball point to point, giving him a large surface on the ball with which to make contact.

An experienced kicker will often make contact directly on the point of the ball, in an attempt to increase height and accuracy. The foot must make contact at the precise point to guarantee success.

4. The Grubber

A Grubber kick projects the ball along the ground, making it roll point over point and eventually causing it to bounce up into the air. This is a particularly useful device to breach a defence that has been tackling well and whose line are moving up quickly. The aim is to kick the ball along the ground between two opposing players, allowing a team mate who is on-side to run through, regain possession and advance the attack.

What to look for (Coaching Points)

a) Hold the ball as if for passing but slightly lower than for the Punt.
b) Keep the eye on the ball.
c) Strike the top of the ball just before it makes contact with the ground.

d) Kick with knee bent and head over the ball.

e) The instep should be stretched down.

f) The foot drives the ball into the ground.

Paul Eastwood grubber kicks, eye on the ball and aiming to strike the top of the ball.

5. The Push Through

This is similar to the Grubber kick but the ball is side footed. The disadvantage is that the ball, when kicked in this way, will not stand up. However, it has the advantage of being;

 a) easier to execute

 b) easier to perform at speed

 c) easier to control the distance at which the ball stops.

What to look for (Coaching Points)

 a) Hold the ball as if for passing.

 b) Keep the eye on the ball.

 c) Strike the ball with the side of the foot immediately it makes contact with the ground.

 d) Contact with the ball should be made when the body is over the ball.

6. The Drop Kick

The Drop kick is made (a) to restart the game from a dead ball situation, or (b) to score a point from the field of play.

What to look for (Coaching Points)

The Drop kick is based on the same principles as the Orthodox punt. The only variation is the timing of the release of the ball which must be such that the foot meets the ball just as it touches the ground.

 a) To start with, look where the kick is to be directed and aim the ball. Then the eyes must concentrate on the area where the foot will connect with the ball.

 b) The head should be down and the eyes kept on the ball until the ball has been kicked.

 c) Hold the ball away from the body. The action should not be cramped by holding the ball too close.

 d) Hold the ball as for a pass and then adjust to an angle from the ground.

 e) Guide the ball to the ground at the same angle without any tilt so that it will hit the ground beside the toes of the non-kicking foot.

 f) With the toe pointing to the ground at approximately the same angle as the ball, kick the ball with the laced part of the boot, not the toe end.

GAINING POSSESSION

The importance of possession in Rugby League cannot be overemphasised. The team who control the ball control the game. The team in opposition can only defend. The various techniques of gaining possession are, therefore, essential for winning Rugby League. Most of the techniques are simple, but all players need to practise them continuously in order to react quickly in pressure situations. Perfect practice will develop a habit so that when the situation arises possession will be yours.

1. Falling on a stationary ball

Because possession is so important, a player under pressure should always be encouraged to play safe and to drop quickly on any loose ball.

What to look for (Coaching Points)

a) The player should move quickly to the ball.

b) Keep the eye on the ball.

c) Fall quickly and decisively next to the ball placing his body between the ball and the opposition, thus shielding the ball.

d) Hold the ball safely in his midriff and curl his body around it.

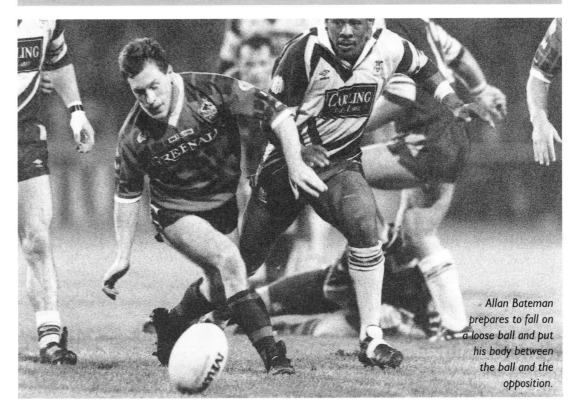

Allan Bateman prepares to fall on a loose ball and put his body between the ball and the opposition.

2. Picking up a stationary ball

If a player is certain that he can pick up a stationary ball safely, he should do so. This will enable him to launch a counter attack which can be productive, especially if the ball has been picked up in open play. It is vital, however, that if there is any doubt in the player's mind of his ability to pick the ball up cleanly, he should play safe, control the ball and drop on it, so securing possession.

What to look for (Coaching Points)

a) The player should move quickly to the ball.

b) Keep the eye on the ball. On approaching the ball, the player should adjust his feet so that they are correctly positioned.

c) Run at the side of the ball.

d) Straddle the ball so that the inner leg is at the back of the ball.

e) Lean the body down close to the ground.

f) If the ball is length ways across, scoop it up with the rear hand going underneath the ball and the other at the front thus preventing a knock-on.

g) If the ball is lying with the point facing the player, he should scoop up the ball by placing the hands at each side of the ball.

The youngster gives an excellent demonstration of picking up a stationary ball.

3. Controlling a moving ball

Because of the shape of a Rugby League ball, it is often difficult to pick up cleanly. All players must be able to control the ball because possession is so vital to achieve success. Players should be encouraged to fall on to a moving ball more often than not, thereby immediately securing possession.

The coaching points – what to look for – for this skill are no different from those already listed.

If time allows, a player can control the ball with his feet, soccer fashion, before picking it up. It is also possible for a player to judge the bounce of the ball and collect it as it bounces in the air.

This skill needs thorough training and should form part of any ball familiarisation exercises under the passing and handling section.

What to look for (Coaching Points)

a) The player should move quickly to the ball.

b) Keep the eye on the ball.

c) On approaching the ball, readjust the feet.

d) Lean the body close to the ground.

e) Extend the hands.

f) Be prepared to catch the ball as it bounces up.

g) Timing is vital.

NB Because possession is so vital, the golden rule is: If in doubt, fall on the ball.

4. Catching a high ball

Because kicking is an important tactic in modern-day Rugby League, all players must be able to catch a ball that has been kicked high into the air.

What to look for (Coaching Points)

a) Concentrate on the ball. Resist the temptation to glance at oncoming opponents.

b) Judge the flight of the ball.

c) Move into position quickly.

d) Keep the eye on the ball.

e) Hold the arms out and up in a searching way with the fingers spread.

f) Allow the ball to land in a cradle formed by the hands, forearms and chest.

g) Trap the ball with hand and forearm as high as possible on the chest.

h) On catching the ball, round the shoulders.

i) Keep the elbows close to the body and close together, bend the knees.

j) The player should turn his side into the opponents, thus giving himself protection and ensuring that the ball cannot be jolted out of his arms in the tackle. By doing this, he will ensure that any dropped ball goes back towards his own posts and is not a knock on.

Alan Tait catches a high ball under the most intense pressure in the 1992 World Cup final.

Progression

As soon as players are proficient catchers, they should be encouraged to perform this skill whilst leaping high into the air. This requires them to move to the ball, and timing again is of vital importance.

Decision making becomes a factor in catching a high ball, as it is not always necessary to take off and leap for a catch when not under pressure.

Pairs Kicking

Skills Developed
The punt kick

Receiving a kick

Level
Beginner/Intermediate/Advanced/All

Explanation

In pairs, partners kick to each other.
Concentrate firstly on technique and accuracy.
Then look at the distance aspect.

1. Accuracy in kicking the ball
    a) to a partner who should not have to move to catch the ball.
    b) between the posts
    c) into a grid or area of the pitch
    d) bouncing into touch.

2. Distance
    a) attempting to force a partner back
    b) start an equal distance from a line and then try to finish closer than the partner.

Variations and Progressions

i) Use the grubber kick.
ii) Use the side-foot push through kick.
iii) Use the chip kick.

Level 2

Over the Top

Skills Developed

Chip kick

Regaining possession

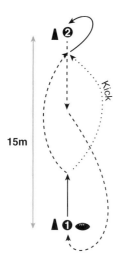

Level

<u>Beginner</u>/<u>Intermediate</u>/Advanced/All

Explanation

Player 1 starts with the ball and advances towards 2.

Player 2 comes forward at the same time.

At the appropriate time, 1 chip kicks over 2 and regathers.

Variations and Progressions

i) Player 1 could advance downfield past a number of defenders.

ii) Defensive pressure can be increased or decreased dependent upon ability.

iii) Support players can be incorporated to regather the kicked ball.

Level 2

Grubber Relay

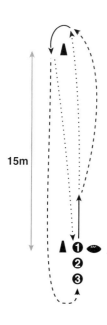

Skills Developed

Grubber kick

Regaining possession

Level

<u>Beginner</u>/Intermediate/Advanced/All

Explanation

Player 1 starts with the ball, advances, grubber kicks, regathers, runs around the marker before grubber kicking the ball to Player 2.

Player 1 then joins the line behind 3.

Player 2 repeats the above.

The drill then continues.

Variations and Progressions

i) On the return grubber kick, the kicker could pressure the receiver.

ii) Use the different kicks, e.g., side-foot, chip kick, etc.

The Chase

Skills Developed

Kicking

Regaining possession

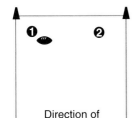

Direction of
movement

Level

Beginner/Intermediate/Advanced/All

Explanation

Players 1 and 2 move down the channel interpassing.
On a given command, the player in possession kicks the ball.
Immediately both kicker and partner chase to safely regather the ball.
NB Ensure all kick variations are used.

Variations and Progressions

i) A defender may be introduced to pressure the kicker or compete for possession.

Catch

Skills Developed   Kicking

Receiving a kick

Level   Beginner/Intermediate/Advanced/<u>All</u>

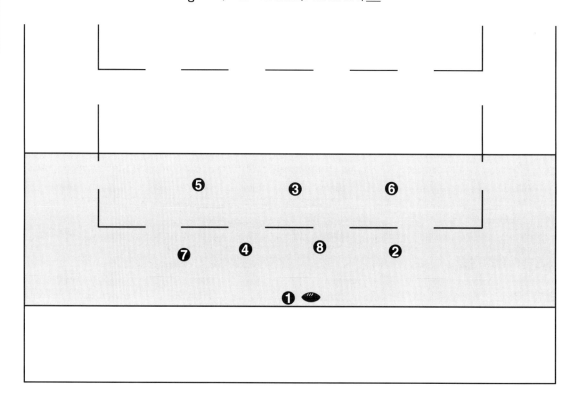

Explanation

A group of players are spread anywhere in the shaded area.

Player 1 kicks the ball high and calls a number.

The player whose number was called must run and catch the kick. He immediately kicks the ball high and calls another number.

Each player has a number of lives and they lose one life (a) for each kick that lands out of bounds, and (b) for each dropped ball.

Variations and Progressions

i) Numbers and size of area.

Kicking Tennis

Skills Developed   Catching a high ball

Chip kicking/bomb kicking

Level   Beginner/<u>Intermediate/Advanced</u>/All

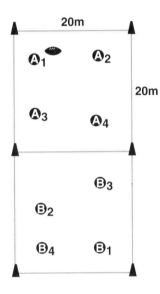

Explanation

Team A start in one grid, Team B in the other.

A1 kicks the ball to land in Team B's grid. Team B attempt to catch the ball cleanly.

B1 then kicks the ball into Team A's grid. Team A attempt to catch the ball cleanly.

A2 then kicks and the game continues.

The kickers score by a ball being allowed to bounce or an error being made by the receivers.

The receivers score if the kickers kick the ball directly out of bounds.

Variations and Progressions

i) Beginners may simply throw a high ball instead of kicking.

ii) Rules may be amended to incorporate grubber kicks.

Kick and Catch

Skills Developed   Chip kick/bomb kicking

Catching

Level   <u>Beginner</u>/<u>Intermediate</u>/Advanced/All

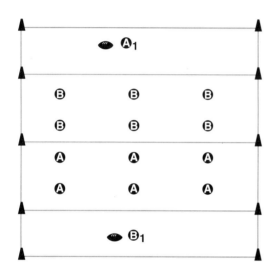

Explanation

A1 and B1 start with a ball each. A1 kicks the ball into the A team section. Any A player catches the ball 'on the full' and kicks it back to A. If A1 catches the ball cleanly, one point is scored. Any error by either player nullifies the point.

B1 starts at the same time as A1 and follows the same sequence. The winners are the team with the most points in a set time.

NB A team members are restricted to their areas as are B team members.

A1 and B1 are restricted to their end zone areas.

Variations and Progressions

i) Have A1 and B1 in a smaller area.

ii) Have A team and B team mixed and moving.

iii) Have A1 and B1 with opposition.

Driving Back

Skills Developed   Kicking

Receiving the ball

Level   Beginner/Intermediate/Advanced/<u>All</u>

Explanation

Players are divided into two equal teams and numbered.

The full pitch is used.

Team A player 1 kicks first from the centre of his 20m line – the rest of his team are onside, i.e., behind the kicker.

Team B have spread out ready to receive the kick.

Upon receiving the ball, Team B player 1 kicks to Team A, then Team A player 2 kicks and so on.

If the ball is caught from the kick 'on the full' (without bouncing) that team are given a 10m bonus, i.e. allowed to bring the ball forward before kicking.

If the receivers knock on they receive a 10m penalty, i.e., take the ball back 10m before kicking.

If the ball is fielded legally after bouncing, the kick is taken from that spot by the player whose turn it is.

If the ball is kicked directly out of play, the other team re-start from where the kick was taken.

If the ball is kicked and bounces into touch (over the sideline) the receiving team kick back from the sideline at the point where the ball crossed out of bounds.

To score a team must kick the ball dead over the in-goal area with a bounce.

Relay Runs

Skills Developed

Picking up a stationary ball

Level

<u>Beginner</u>/Intermediate/Advanced/All

Explanation

Player 1 starts with the ball, runs to the mid-point, places the ball on the ground and continues to behind Player 4.

As soon as the ball is placed on the ground, Player 2 advances, picks up and runs with the ball before passing to Player 3.

Player 3 then runs to the mid-point, places the ball and the drill continues.

Variations and Progressions

i) After stationary ball pick up move on to:

Falling on to a stationary ball.

Moving ball.

Hand on pass.

Throwing high into the air.

Possession Gain Pairs

Skills Developed

Picking up a moving ball

Receiving a high ball

Level

Beginner/Intermediate/Advanced/All

Explanation

Two players working together a short distance apart (approx 10m).

One player feeds the ball and the other gains possession.

Pressure can be developed by the feeder following the ball in and offering some form of opposition.

The opposition needs to be almost passive at first, but gradually increased as the receiver becomes more proficient.

Mix up rolling, bouncing and throwing a high ball as the feed.

Pick up from the side

Skills Developed

Picking up a moving ball

Level

Beginner/Intermediate/Advanced/All

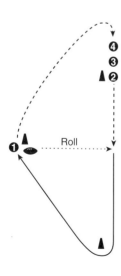

Explanation

Player 1 starts with the ball and rolls it from the side as shown, then joins the line behind Player 4.

As soon as the ball is rolled, Player 2 advances and picks the ball up, continues round the cone to the side where he rolls the ball.

The drill continues.

Variations and Progressions

i) Rolling from the other side.

ii) Altering the side cone so that the ball is rolled from a different angle.

iii) Speeding up the roll.

iv) Rolling from directly in front of the receiver.

v) Rolling from the same point as the receiver.

Quick Score

Skills developed   Regaining possession

Evasive skills

Ball carrying

Level   <u>Beginner</u>/Intermediate/Advanced/All

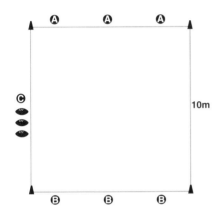

10m

Explanation

Players and coach commence as shown in the diagram.

The coach (C) rolls or kicks three balls into the grid.

Team A gathers the balls, one each, and then attempts to 'score' at the opposite side of the grid. The ball is held in two hands whilst running.

Team B may 'harass' team A, but not grab them.

The roles are reversed.

The winner is the team which takes less time for all players to 'score'.

Variations and Progressions

i) Coach can commence game by throwing high balls into the grid.

High Ball Gauntlet

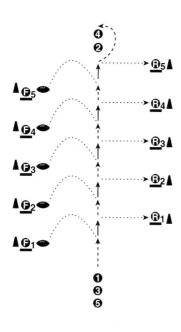

Skills Developed

Catching a high ball

Level

Beginner/<u>Intermediate/Advanced</u>/All

Explanation

Markers are staggered as in diagram with each feeder (F) having a ball.

F1 throws a high ball into the corridor, Player 1 advances and catches the ball before giving an onside pass to Receiver 1 (R1).

He then progresses down the corridor, catching each feeder's throw before passing to the corresponding receiver.

After finishing the gauntlet, he joins the back of the line at Player 4. Player 2 then runs the gauntlet in the other direction.

The drill is continuous.

Variations and Progressions

i) Ensure the ball is fed from both left and right.

ii) The angle of throw can be varied.

iii) If the feeders are skilled enough, and by amending the distances, a kick can be used.

iv) Pressure can be increased by the feeder then challenging the receiver.

v) The ball can be rolled or bounced into the corridor by the feeder.

vi) Numbers can be amended depending on group size.

SCRUMMAGING

Description

In modern-day Rugby League, the scrum is simply more and more a means by which to restart play and the team who have had a break down in skill, i.e., by knocking-on, forward pass, etc, or having kicked over the sideline for territory gain, are penalised and possession tends to go to the team who feed the scrum.

However, it is vital that the players pack down in a technically correct manner in order to ensure that such possession is not squandered through poor technique, or that the team who are feeding the ball are not pushed off possession.

Furthermore, a technically correct formation allows for a good channel of the ball in order to bring the backs into play with an efficient pass from the base of the scrum.

A scrum in Rugby League usually consists of six players packing in a 3, 2, 1 formation.

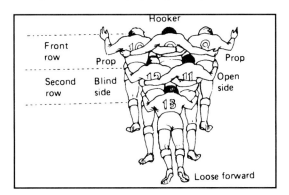

The pack consists of three players in the front row who by interlocking their arms and heads with their opponents form a clear tunnel at right angles to the touchline. The open-side prop forward should stand at the side of the scrum which is next to the referee as this is where the ball will be put in. The man in the middle is the hooker who is supported on each side by the prop forwards. It is his task to channel the ball backwards when the ball is fed into the scrum by his team.

Two second row forwards pack down behind the front row and are bound together by their arms, gripping each other's bodies. Their heads are placed in the two gaps between the hooker and the props.

The loose forward packs down behind the second row forwards with his head in between them.

The upper bodies of all the forwards should be horizontal to the ground.

When the scrummage has been correctly formed, the forwards take the weight and hold the scrum on the mark until the ball is put in.

The scrum half feeds the ball into the tunnel by rolling it along the ground and the hooker is allowed to strike the ball with either foot once it has made contact with the ground in the tunnel. A good strike from the hooker accompanied by a forceful push from the entire pack will ensure that the ball emerges from between the inner feet of the second row forwards, allowing the side in possession to launch an attack.

Importance of Possession

Scrummaging is still an important contributary factor to possession, and possession in Rugby League football is probably more important than in any other team game.

Coaches can therefore conclude that their team should:

a) win every scrum when they have the head;
b) reduce the number of scrum penalties conceded;
and
c) attempt in vital positions to push the opposition off the ball at least once per game.

To achieve these objectives, a team needs to develop the skill of efficient scrummaging within the Laws of the Game.

Major Principles of Scrummaging

The abilities required to achieve the above objectives are:

1. To push the hooker closer to the ball than the opposition's hooker.
2. To create a good striking position while at the same time making difficulties for the opposition.
3. To push over the ball and push the opposition off it.

The major principles of scrummaging are therefore: scrum formation, a quick strike for the ball and a strong coordinating push.

Formation of the Scrum

What to look for (Coaching Points)

All forwards
a) The hooker should try to be the first to arrive at the mark of the scrum.
b) The rest of the pack should follow quickly and form up before the opposition.

Front Row

a) The props position themselves beside the hooker with the open-side prop standing at the side of the referee.

b) To assist the hooker it is an advantage if the open-side prop is taller than the blind-side prop. The position is made easier if the blind-side prop packs in a lower position than the open-side prop. By doing this the hooker is naturally turned towards the put in and has a better view of the ball coming in.

c) The heads and the bodies of the three front-row forwards should be close together.

d) The open-side prop should place his inside shoulder behind that of his hooker.

e) He should grasp either (i) the shirt of the blind-side prop firmly under the shoulder, commonly used if the hooker is strongly built (see diagram), or (ii) the hip of the hooker and help to pull him over the ball particularly if the hooker is slightly built (see diagram).

f) The blind-side prop has his inside shoulder pushing into the armpit of his hooker and grasps the shirt of the open-side prop firmly under the armpit. This binding gives the blind-side prop the longest possible extension of his arm to assist in pushing his hooker over the ball.

g) The hooker binds over the shoulders of the two prop forwards.

h) The front row should on no account go down into the scrum until the second row is securely in position.

Second Row.

a) The two second-row forwards bind firmly together before entering the scrum.

b) The open-side second-row forward should bind over the arm of the blind-side second row, who should have his arm under the arm of the open side second row.

c) The second row forwards should not disturb the front row and must move into position lower down with their heads going into the gaps between the hooker and props.

d) The second row's shoulders should be moved up so they rest under the natural bulge of the props buttocks.

e) Both second row's backs should be straight and parallel to the ground to ensure a flat back, while the head is kept up locking the back in a strong, straight, safe position.

f) The second row forwards should help bind the front row tight.

Loose Forward (see diagram).

a) The loose forward should place his head between the two second row forwards.

b) The loose forward's shoulders should rest underneath the natural bulge of the second row's buttocks.

c) The loose forward's back should be straight and parallel to the ground in a strong, safe pushing position.

d) The loose forward's arms should encircle the two second row forwards and bind them securely together.

Striking for the Ball

a) The formation of the scrum should take into account the individual preferences of the hooker, holding him in a position to enable him to strike quickly.

b) The formation of the scrum should also push the hooker as close as possible to the point of entry of the ball.

c) It is an advantage for the hooker to strike for the ball with the near foot because that is the closest to the ball.

There are two actions:

i) Raking action – see diagram. The hooker bends the knee closest to the put in and reaches over the ball, raking it back with his heel. The action is similar to riding a bicycle.

ii) Striking action – see diagram. A faster action in which the hooker strikes straight ahead hitting the ground with his heel and immediately turning the foot outwards around the ball. With practice the ball will be directed through the scrum in a straight line.

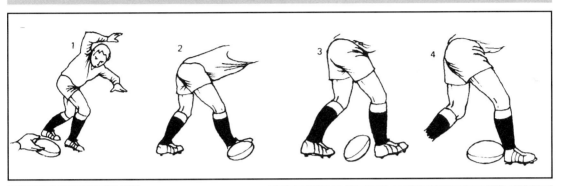

d) Hookers using the far foot have their weight on the near foot and have to rake the ball back with a swinging action – see diagram.

Advantages of far foot hooking – inexperienced players will often have more control over the ball.

Disadvantages of far foot hooking – the hooker immediately loses any advantages of having the head and is at an even greater disadvantage when the opposition has it. He has to turn his body to face out towards the ball and runs the risk of being penalised for not packing square.

e) Hookers should be discouraged from squatting as this will slow their hooking action, particularly when being pinned down by the weight of the opposition's front row.

The Push

a) The pack should attempt to form up before the opposition but they should not form the scrum until all their forwards are in position.

b) All the forwards should be aware of their duties and should concentrate on them. Possession is important and the scrum is no place to have a rest.

c) The pack should attempt to push the hooker over the ball at the earliest legal moment. The push should be a single force towards the opposing front row. In order to achieve this concerted force, attention must be paid to the following:

   i) The forwards must be parallel. Any forward out of line is wasting his effort and is unable to transmit in the right direction the force applied by the players behind him.

   ii) The upper bodies of the pack must be as near horizontal as possible with their backs flat and parallel with the ground.

   iii) A forward pushing with a rounded back is not only in a weak position, but will also hinder the pushing of the other forwards.

   iv) All the forwards must push at the same time.

d) The second row should push the hooker towards the ball. It helps if the taller of the two second row forwards packs down behind the open-side prop forward and places his arm over that of the blind-side second row.

e) The blind-side second row with his arm under the open-side second row is able to place his inside shoulder under the hooker's buttocks and push him over the ball.

f) The position of the feet is very important (see diagram on next page). The open-side prop forward

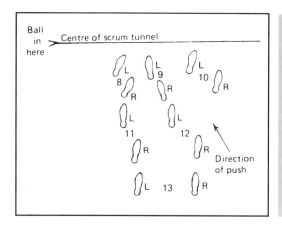

should have his nearest foot forward to keep his hooker on side. His furthest foot, the pushing foot, is placed slightly behind the front. The hooker should position himself so that his striking foot is slightly forward. The blind-side prop forward should have his non-pushing foot next to the hooker, forward and touching the centre of the scrum. This furthest pushing foot is placed to the side and back in line with the heel of his inside foot. In this way the prop's near-side hip is able to give strong support to the hooker.

g) The second row should push with their furthest legs back.

h) The loose forward's feet are spread for pushing and balance.

Partner Scrummaging

Skills Developed   Scrummaging position

Level   <u>Beginner</u>/Intermediate/Advanced/All

Explanation

Two players in a safe and strong scrummaging position compete against one another. They have chins lifted and backs flat, with feet spread out, and each grips his partner's jersey at the shoulders while endeavouring to pull or push him off balance.

Children should be with those of a similar size.

Scrum Half/Hooker Strike

Skills Developed	Correct feeding of the scrum
	Striking for the ball

Level Beginner/Intermediate/Advanced/All

Explanation

The hooker faces forward, with the scrum half to his side. The scrum half is holding the ball and facing the hooker.

The Scrum Half:

Bends down holding the ball, point to point, close to the ground.

Rolls the ball along the ground, in front of the hooker.

Quickly retires behind the hooker.

Picks up the ball when it appears.

The Hooker:

Bends forward with head turned to concentrate on the ball.

Strikes for the ball – practise the different techniques.

Diverts the ball backwards.

Ensure the ball is put in from both sides. It is an idea for the hooker to have passive opposition to hold on to.

Scrum Half/Front Row

Skills Developed	Correct binding of the front row
	Correct feeding of the scrum
	Striking for the ball

Level Beginner/Intermediate/Advanced/All

Explanation

The front row binds in the appropriate manner against a passive opposition front three.

The scrum half feeds the ball in the correct manner.

Levels 2 and 3

The hooker strikes and diverts the ball backwards.

Ensure practice from both sides.

Children should be evenly matched.

Variations and Progressions

i) At the appropriate point, introduce a more realistic opposition.

Scrum Half/Pack

Skills Developed

Correct binding of the scrum

Correct foot positioning

Correct feeding of the scrum

Striking for the ball

Level

Beginner/Intermediate/Advanced/<u>All</u>

Explanation

A pack of forwards pack down against a passive front row. Scrum half correctly feeds the ball. The ball is channelled out of the scrum in a controlled manner. Ensure practice from both sides. Children should be evenly matched.

Variations and Progressions

i) Practise against a full pack

TACKLING AND DEFENCE

One of the most important tackles of the 1995 World Cup – Tim Brasher halts England's Barrie Jon Mather with a superb side tackle

Tackling is a vital individual skill.

All players should include tackling practice as part of their weekly programme.

Players need to adopt a positive attitude to tackling.

The American football philosophy of attacking through defence should be the approach, and the aim of most tackles should be not merely to stop the other side's progress, but to go forward and attempt to gain possession by forcing the ball carrier into handling errors. This mental attitude to the defensive aspect of the game is vital.

Players should be encouraged to think 'go forward at all times' whether in possession of the ball or without the ball.

However, a player should first of all become proficient in the techniques of all the various tackles and needs to be coached in such a way that he finds this aspect of the game enjoyable.

Coaches should attempt to develop technically proficient players in all aspects of tackling. The players need to be taught correctly at a very early stage of their development.

The coaching needs to be positive at all times and emphasis should be placed on the pleasure that can be obtained from executing a full-blooded tackle rather than any mention of injury or fear.

Players enjoy tackling as long as the ground and weather conditions are suitable they are in groups of equal age and size and the practice is relatively short.

Side Tackle

The side tackle is the easiest to execute and for this reason should be introduced first.

What to look for (Coaching Points)

a) The player should tackle with determination.
b) Keep eyes on the target – the thigh.
c) The head of the tackler should be behind the ball carrier at all times.
d) The shoulder should make contact and drive powerfully into the target.
e) The arms should strongly encircle the thighs and grip tight.
f) The tackler should hold the ball carrier until he is well and truly tackled and on the ground.
g) The tackler should finish on top of the ball carrier.

The Front Tackle

Tackling head on is vital to team play.

Coaches should ensure that all their players are introduced to the techniques of the front tackle and then encouraged to practise.

A player who is reluctant to tackle head on is always suspect when playing against faster opposition and will cause untold problems in team play if he persistently manoeuvres the ball carrier into a position in which he can perform a side tackle.

There are two types of head on tackles:

1) **Block**. When the tackler uses the momentum of the ball carrier and blocks the ball carrier.
2) **Blockbuster**. When the tackler forcefully knocks the ball carrier backwards.

Front Block Tackle

This is easier to execute than the blockbuster. It is used most often when the ball carrier is larger than the tackler and is approaching at speed. The aim is to encircle his legs quickly and use his momentum to bring him down.

What to look for (Coaching Points)

a) The player should keep his eyes on the target – the thighs.

b) Position the body so that the head and neck are to the side of the ball carrier.

c) Use the ball carrier's own weight and momentum to make the tackle.

d) The tackler should hit the thighs of the ball carrier with his shoulders.

e) The arms should powerfully encircle the legs and grip tight.

f) The ball carrier should be rolled on to his side.

g) The tackler should finish on top of the tackled player.

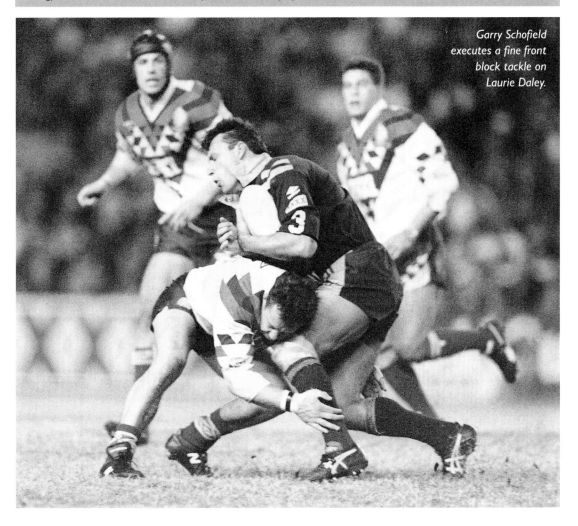

Garry Schofield executes a fine front block tackle on Laurie Daley.

The Blockbuster

With the blockbuster, the tackler must move quickly into position and contact is usually made before the ball carrier has had time to build up a momentum. By positioning the feet, driving powerfully and lifting, the opponent is forcefully knocked over backwards. The target area for this tackle is slightly below the ball and timing is the key to success.

What to look for (Coaching Points)

a) The player should be determined.

b) The shoulder should drive powerfully into the target area.

c) Keep eyes on the target just below the ball.

d) Drive powerfully forward, the head of the tackler should be to the side of the ball.

e) The arms should powerfully encircle the ball carrier below the centre of gravity, that is, below the buttocks, and grip tightly.

f) Drive powerfully with the legs.

g) Pull and lift with the arms and shoulders.

h) Drive the ball carrier upwards and then backwards.

i) Finish on top of the ball carrier with the shoulder buried into the target area.

j) Timing is the key.

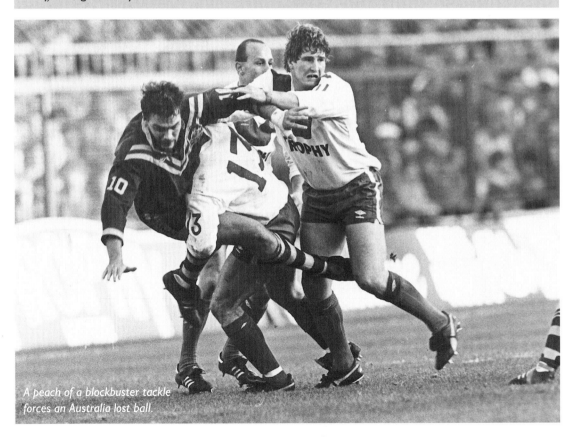

A peach of a blockbuster tackle forces an Australia lost ball.

The Rear Tackle

It is essential that all players practise this tackle because, when the line has been broken, the rear tackle is the one most commonly employed when defences are scrambling back in order to prevent a score.

What to look for (Coaching Points)

  a) The player should tackle with determination.
  b) Keep eyes on the target – the thigh.
  c) The head of the tackler should always be to the side of the ball carrier.
  d) The shoulder should make contact and drive powerfully into the target.
  e) The arms should strongly encircle the thighs and grip tightly.
  f) The tackler should finish on top of the ball carrier.

The Smother Tackle

This type of tackle, also commonly known as the 'ball and all' tackle, should only be introduced when players are fully proficient at tackling hard and low. Team players who develop the habit of persistently

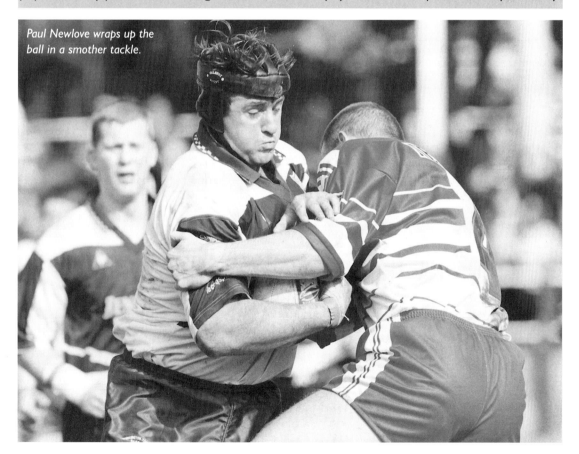

Paul Newlove wraps up the ball in a smother tackle.

tackling high should be quickly discouraged. Occasionally, however, a smother tackle can be most effective, especially when the tackler is left facing a ball carrier who has support or if the tackler knows that there will be numbers available to support him in the tackle.

What to look for (Coaching Points)

a) The player should tackle with determination.

b) Keep the eyes on the target – the player with the ball.

c) Move forward into position quickly.

d) Pin the ball between the body of the tackler and the ball carrier.

e) The arms should be powerfully wrapped around the upper part of the ball carrier's body.

f) The arms of the ball carrier must be trapped to his sides.

g) The ball carrier should be forced to the ground whenever possible.

h) Timing is again vital.

The emphasis is on power, determination and timing.

One on one or two on one actual tackle technique work with players is vital if players are to achieve adequate technique. However, other training equipment is available to assist all aspects of defensive work. These are tackle shields/hit shields, tackle bags, body armour (where the players are strapped into the padding) and inner tubes.

Rugby League more than any other sport requires all players to have a solid defence. Individual tackling technique is, therefore, most important. Coaches should ensure that all players under their guidance are proficient in all forms of tackling. He must spend time observing, analysing and improving each player individually.

More often than not players needing improvement should tackle other players, but for competent tacklers or at certain times of the week or training year, drills on shields and tackle bags would be more beneficial.

When improving individual defence the coach should concentrate on;

a) technique as above

b) balance and footwork – the defender must be agile and capable of moving quickly into the tackle, and his footwork should be monitored closely with his tackling technique

c) head down – the player's chin should be close to his chest, eyes observing the opposition as he gets ready to hit. It is an idea for the players to be given the picture of looking over their glasses when making a tackle

d) shoulder contact – the shoulder should always make contact being driven with determination into the target area

e) tackle low – the first man into the tackle should always tackle low, thrusting his shoulder into the target area to ensure that the ball carrier is stopped and quickly grounded

and

f) timing of the tackle is an important consideration – players must concentrate on this aspect of defending.

Defensive Organisation

Drills and small-sided games can be used to improve this aspect of defence. Communication, understanding, physical conditioning and commitment are essential ingredients of successful defensive play. The first step is to understand fully the following aspects of defensive organisation.

a) Individual tackling skill – see above.

b) The defensive line.

c) Positional play in the defensive line.

d) The marker defence.

e) The sweeper.

f) The two man tackle.

g) The gang tackle.

h) Controlling the collision, i.e., the speed at which the opposition play the ball.

i) Equating in numbers.

j) The speed of the line.

k) Cover/scramble defence.

l) Goal-line defence.

These ingredients of successful defensive organisation need also to be fully understood by all of the players and practised via drills and games so that appropriate responses become habitual.

Introductory Tackling

Skills Developed   All appropriate tackles in a safe environment

Level   Beginner/Intermediate/Advanced/All

Explanation

In pairs, using the natural progression and checking correct, appropriate technique.

1. Tackler kneeling, ball carrier stationary.

2. Tackler kneeling, ball carrier walking.

3. Tackler crouching, ball carrier walking.

4. Tackler standing, ball carrier walking.

5. Tackler walking, ball carrier walking.

6. Tackler standing, ball carrier jogging.

7. Tackler walking, ball carrier jogging.

8. Tackler jogging, ball carrier jogging.

NB Ensure the ball carrier has a ball.

Variations and Progressions

i) In pairs, with players facing one another two metres apart, 1 tackles 2 who is carrying a ball.

Both regain their feet, return to original position and the drill continues with the tackler attempting to make a maximum number of tackles in a given time.

Then alternate the pairs.

Right Angle

Skills Developed   Side tackle

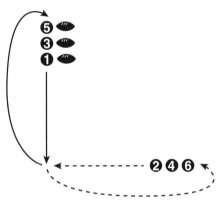

Level
Beginner/Intermediate/Advanced/All

Explanation

Players are arranged as shown.

1, 3 and 5 carry a ball.

Player 1 advances, at the same time 2 starts, times his run and executes a technically correct side tackle.

Both players regain their feet, 1 hands the ball to 2 and joins the line at the back of 6, 2 joins the line at the back of 5.

Player 3 then advances and 4 tackles and so the drill continues.

Variations and Progressions

i) Ensure both left shoulder side tackle and right shoulder side tackle is practised.

ii) Speed can be increased when appropriate.

Tackle Square

Skills Developed   Front block tackle
Conditioning

Level   Beginner/Intermediate/Advanced/All

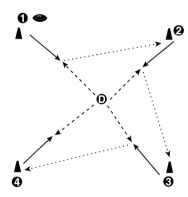

Explanation

Players 1 to 4 are positioned at the markers as shown.

Defender D stands in the middle of the grid.

Player 1 starts with the ball and progresses towards the centre of the grid. Defender advances and tackles him.

Player 1 regains his feet and passes to Player 2, Defender returns to the middle of the grid.

Player 2 then progresses towards the centre, the Defender advances and tackles him and the drill continues for one minute.

One on One Chase

Skills Developed   Rear tackle

Level   Beginner/Intermediate/Advanced/All

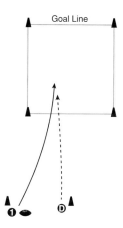

Explanation

Ball carrier (Player 1) sets off into the grid with the intention of crossing the goal-line to score. This is on the coach's command.

As soon as 1 sets off, Defender (D) chases and effects a tackle.

Make sure the ball carrier sets off to both the left and the right of the defender.

Variations and Progressions

i) Numbers of attackers and/or defenders can be varied to simulate the situation that the coach desires.

ii) Differing angles of run by the attacker into the grid.

Introduction to Tackle Shields

Skills Developed Safety when using a shield

10m

Level
Beginner/Intermediate/Advanced/All

Explanation

Player 1 and Player 2 holding the shield commence jogging towards each other.

The shield should be held firmly with both arms through the two straps at the back and in front of the chest and abdomen.

At the point of impact, both players must brace their body, have both feet firmly on the ground, lean forcefully into the opposition and watch their partners.

Player 1 must hit with the shoulder, place both arms around the opposition and drive with the legs after impact.

Run the Channel

Skills Developed Tackling
Evasive skills

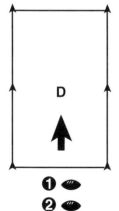

Level
Beginner/Intermediate/Advanced/All

Explanation

Players begin as shown.

The defender's task is to halt the ball carrier.

Player 1 advances and after either being tackled or reaching the end of the channel, Player 2 advances and so on.

In a set time count the number of tackles before changing the defender.

Variations and Progressions

i) The width of the channel

– narrower to advantage the defender

– wider to disadvantage the defender

ii) Two or more defenders spaced equally along the channel.

'X' Tackling

Skills Developed   Tackling

Level   Beginner/<u>Intermediate</u>/Advanced/All

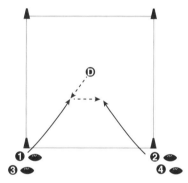

Explanation

Players line up as shown in the diagram

Player 1 carrying a ball advances and tries to cross diagonally to the opposite cone.

The defender (D) attempts to prevent this.

After the first tackle Player 2 enters the grid trying to cross diagonally to the opposite cone and so on.

The drill is continuous for a set time or a number of tackles.

Ensure all players defend and use both left and right shoulder.

Variations and Progressions

i) As proficiency in defence increases, so should the tempo of the attackers.

ii) Two defenders can be used.

Level 2

Pressure Tackling

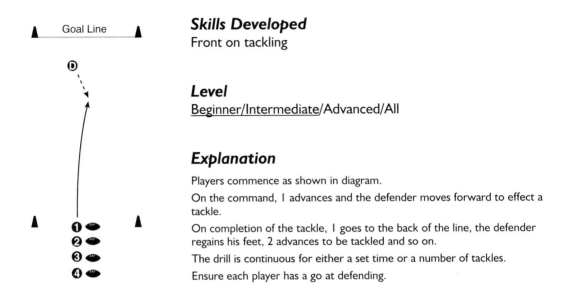

Skills Developed
Front on tackling

Level
<u>Beginner/Intermediate</u>/Advanced/All

Explanation
Players commence as shown in diagram.

On the command, 1 advances and the defender moves forward to effect a tackle.

On completion of the tackle, 1 goes to the back of the line, the defender regains his feet, 2 advances to be tackled and so on.

The drill is continuous for either a set time or a number of tackles.

Ensure each player has a go at defending.

Variations and Progressions

i) As proficiency in defence increases, the attackers' tempo should also increase.

ii) Two defenders can be staggered in the channel so that if the attacker evades the first challenge, he has to work even harder to cross the goal-line.

Level 2

Round the Cone Tackling

Skills Developed
Front on tackling

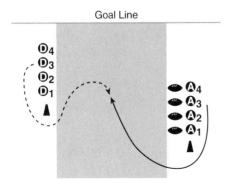

Level
<u>Beginner/Intermediate</u>/Advanced/All

Explanation
Players commence as in the diagram.

Attackers (A's) have a ball.

The coach calls a number, e.g. 3, and both A3 (attacker) and D3 (defender) sprint round the appropriate cone into the shaded channel.

Attackers attempt to score over the goal-line and defenders attempt to effect a tackle.

Ensure all players attack and defend

Variations and Progressions

i) Make sure defenders defend from both right and left.

ii) Vary the position of cones to ensure the different types of tackle, e.g., rear, front.

Robbers 3 v 1

Level 1

Skills Developed   Tackling technique

Level   <u>Beginner</u>/Intermediate/Advanced/All

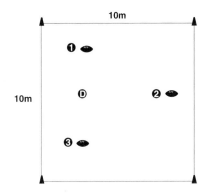

Explanation

The players are set out as shown in the diagram.

Players 1, 2 and 3 are carrying a ball and attempting to evade the defender.

The defender has to tackle the ball carriers in any order as quickly as possible.

The defender has one minute maximum to complete the task.

After a ball carrier has been tackled he should leave the grid.

NB Ensure correct technique at all times for safety.

3 v 2 Bulldog

Skills Developed   Tackling

Level   Beginner/<u>Intermediate</u>/Advanced/All

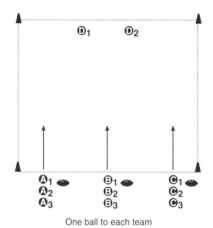

One ball to each team

Explanations

One ball to each team.

On the command 'Go' all the attacking teams (A, B and C) set off with the objective being to cross the opposite grid boundary and score a try within the rules of Rugby League. The defending pair (D1 and D2) attempt to complete a tackle or force an error.

When a team fail to score or make an error, they are eliminated. The winners are the last team to score a try.

Variations and Progressions

i) Using shields rather than a full tackle.

4 v 4 Zone Defence

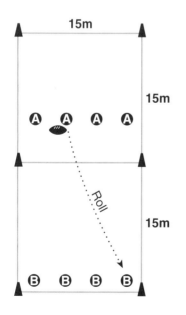

Skills Developed

Maintaining the defensive line

Zone defence

Decision making in defence

Communication

Level

Beginner/Intermediate/<u>Advanced</u>/All

Explanation

Players start as shown.

Team A roll the ball to team B.

B then commence attacking. B team have six tackles to score.

The coach encourages the attackers to use drop offs, run-rounds etc.

Team A defend using a zone defence and a two-handed touch.

Upon being tackled (touched) all defenders retire 5 m and the attackers restart with a pass.

After one team has had five sets of tackles in attack, alternate the roles.

The defence should move up and slide across together to control the game.

Line Discipline

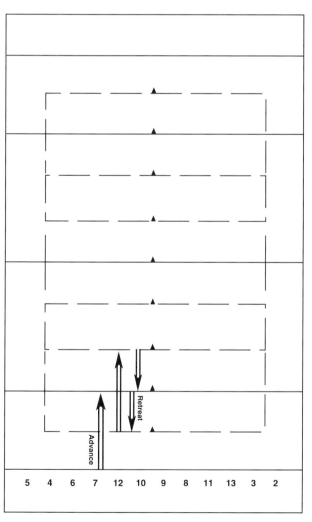

Skills Developed

Organisation

Communication

Level

Beginner/Intermediate/Advanced/<u>All</u>

Explanation

Markers are set out at 10m intervals down the field (as shown).

Players commence on the goal-line.

On a given command all the players advance, two markers fall to the ground and then retreat one cone.

The drill continues as such the full length of the pitch.

NB Ensure the line advances as one.

Variations and Progressions

i) The coach stands 20m in front of the line and the defence have to respond to his signals, i.e., moving forward, backwards, sliding, shuffling, dropping to the ground, rolling etc.

ii) The players are split into two equal groups, one group with tackle shields, standing on the first marker facing the other group (the tacklers).

The tacklers advance, hit the shields with good defensive technique and drive the shields backwards to the next marker.

The tacklers then retreat 10m.

This sequence is repeated down the pitch.

Ensure the line advances as one.

Defensive Line Positioning

Skills Developed	Organisation
	Communication

Level	Beginner/<u>Intermediate</u>/<u>Advanced</u>/All

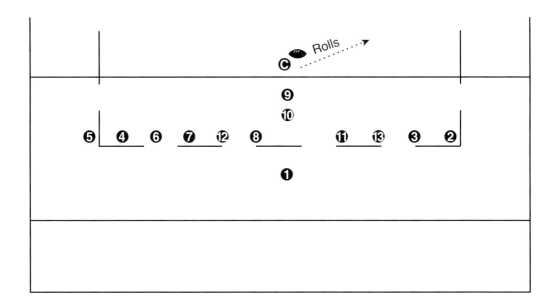

Explanation

Players line up as a team in their appropriate defensive line positions (diagram is simply a suggestion).

Coach who starts with the ball rolls it anywhere on the field.

The defensive line advances and the two nearest defenders drop on the ball.

This represents a tackle.

Meanwhile the rest of the defensive line should re-position themselves accordingly.

The full-back (Player 1) should communicate with the line to ensure there are no obvious gaps.

The ball is then given back to the coach in a new position and the sequence commences again.

NB Ensure that the coach varies the distance and angle of the roll.

Variations and Progression

i) Play a defensive set of six tackles in all different parts of the playing area.

ii) Play a defensive set of six tackles from taps, scrums, etc.

iii) Ensure all players know their positions and roles to play in all conceivable defensive situations.

iv) Instead of the coach rolling a ball, have the defenders play two-handed touch or grip against conditioned opposition.

Re-alignment

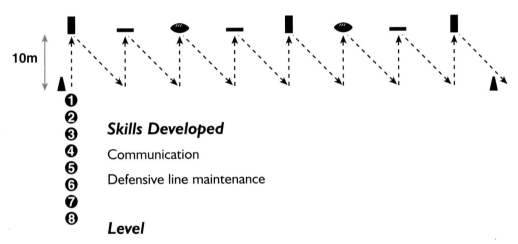

10m

① ② ③ ④ ⑤ ⑥ ⑦ ⑧

Skills Developed

Communication

Defensive line maintenance

Level

Beginner/<u>Intermediate</u>/<u>Advanced</u>/All

Explanation

The players and equipment commence as shown.

Player 1 advances, hits the tackle bag and retreats diagonally.

Player 2 then joins the defensive line and both advance to hit the tackle bag or shield before retreating diagonally so that 1, 2 and 3 are hitting a bag, shield or falling on a loose ball.

This continues until they are all working together.

The drill is complete when Player 8 has passed the second marker cone.

Variations and Progressions

i) Dependent upon equipment.

Level 3

Reaction

Skills Developed

Defensive communication

Alignment

Level

Beginner/<u>Intermediate/Advanced</u>/All

Explanation

The squad are divided into two equal groups and commence as in the diagram.

The coach (C) stands behind the defenders and controls the movement of the attackers (players 1 to 4) who are holding tackle shields, whilst the defenders (D1 to D4) react to their movement.

When the coach indicates right, the offence follows him and the defenders react accordingly.

When the coach moves his hands upwards, the offence moves forward, and the defenders move up in a line to tackle the shields with good technique.

The defenders release upon instruction, the two lines retreat and the drill continues for six tackles.

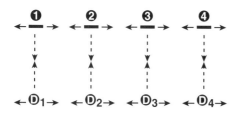

Level 3

Unequal Numbers

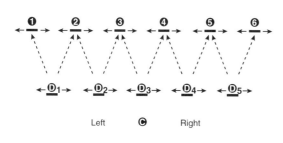

Left   C   Right

Skills Developed

Communication

Defensive alignment

Level

Beginner/Intermediate/<u>Advanced</u>/All

Explanation

This drill is built upon the reaction drill featured previously.

The squad are divided into unequal numbers (e.g., 6 and 5).

The coach (C) stands behind the defenders and controls the movement of the attackers who are holding tackle shields (Players 1 to 6) whilst the defenders (D1 to D5) react to their movements as in the Reaction Drill.

However, if the Coach has indicated to his right and has then signalled for the attackers to advance, D5 should tackle Player 6, D4 Player 5, D3 Player 4, D2 Player 3, D1 Player 2, leaving Player 1 free.

If the Coach has indicated to his left and has then signalled advances, D1 should tackle Player 1, D2 Player 2 and so on.

In other words, if the last indication before advance is right, the defenders should slide right as a unit and if the last indication before advance is left, then the defenders should slide left as a unit.

The only player left free should be the end player.

Each defender is responsible for either of two attackers (as in diagram) and he should identify to the other defenders which he is to tackle.

The defenders release upon instruction, the two lines retreat and the drill continues for six tackles.

Variations and Progressions

i) As the defenders become proficient, mix up the instructions, e.g., left, right, left, advance, etc.

ii) Add a further defender as sweeper approx. 5m behind the defensive line to tackle the spare end player who advances.

iii) A further instruction is added 'change'. Upon hearing this the end attackers should move from their position and re-join the attackers wherever they wish.

This will force the defenders to re-identify who they have to slide on to.

Front Marker Check and Chase

Level 3

Skills Developed   Marker defence

Level   Beginner/<u>Intermediate</u>/<u>Advanced</u>/All

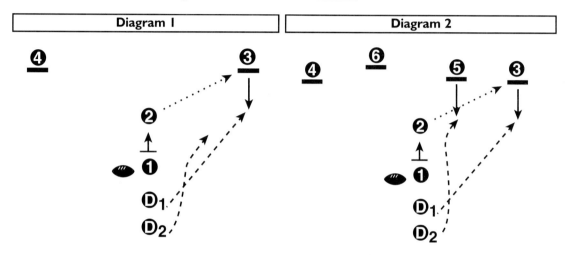

Diagram 1	Diagram 2

Explanation

To commence, start as in Diagram 1.

Player 1 plays the ball to Player 2 who then rolls or passes the ball in the direction of either Player 3 or 4.

In Diagram 1 the ball is passed/rolled towards Player 3 holding a tackle shield. He disregards the ball but advances as if carrying it.

The first marker (D1) checks that the dummy half has not run with the ball (Player 2) and on seeing the ball rolled/passed chases in that direction to tackle the first receiver (Player 3).

The second marker (D2) momentarily waits before following D1 on the inside (as shown) and assisting in tackling the first receiver (player 3).

NB Practise with ball being rolled/passed both to the right and left.

At all times D1 checks the dummy half before chasing after the ball and D2 waits before following.

To further advance the drill encourage Player 2 to pick the ball up and run. If this happens D1 should be able to adjust and tackle the runner with assistance from D2.

Insist that D1 'name drops' the dummy half so that the dummy half is aware that the markers are checking on him before chasing.

In Diagram 2 a further attacking option is incorporated, the inside ball.

Player 1 plays the ball to 2, 2 rolls/passes to either right or left.

In Diagram 2, the ball goes in the direction of Players 3 and 5. Both players disregard the ball but advance, Player 3 as first receiver and Player 5 slightly later as if being passed an inside ball.

In this instance the first marker (D1) checks the dummy half, then chases the ball to tackle the first receiver (Player 3). The second marker (D2) momentarily waits before following D1 on the inside which allows him to tackle Player 5.

Again practise to the right and left and also with the dummy half picking the ball up and running.

Variations and Progressions

i) Same practices but with the roles at marker reversed, i.e., the second marker D2 checks and chases (<u>Back Marker Check and Chase</u>).

ii) <u>Front Marker Fly</u> – players commence as in Diagram 1 but the front marker (D1) disregards the dummy half and anticipates the direction of the pass. Then as soon as the ball is played D1 flies towards the first receiver to pressurise him. The second marker (D2) holds, checks the dummy half for running off and, if the ball is passed, chases after the ball.

iii) <u>Back Marker Fly</u> – as in (ii) except that the roles are reversed and the back marker (D2) anticipates and flies at the first receiver to pressurise him.

iv) <u>Two Step</u> - players commence as in Diagram 1 but the back marker (D2) communicates with the front marker (D1) and tells him to step right/left when the ball is played. D1 responds accordingly and D2 steps the opposite way.

If D1 steps right and the ball goes right he should chase the ball, and D2 after stepping left should then follow D1 and pick up any inside plays.

If D1 steps right, D2 steps left and the ball goes left, D2 becomes chaser and D1 steps right and then follows to pick up any inside plays.

If the dummy half runs, whichever marker steps in that direction should pick him up and tackle him.

v) <u>Think Right/Think Left</u> – players commence as in Diagram 1. The back marker (D2) communicates with the front marker (D1) and instructs him to either think right/think left.

If D1 is thinking right and the ball goes right, he chases towards the first receiver and D2 then follows on the inside.

If D1 is thinking right and the ball goes left, D2 chases towards the first receiver and D1 then follows on the inside.

If the dummy half runs right D1 thinking right should tackle him; if he is running left D2 who is thinking left tackles him.

THERE ARE MANY VARIATIONS OF MARKER PLAY – AS A COACH, SELECT WHAT YOU FEEL IS THE MOST APPROPRIATE AND PERFECT IT THROUGH PRACTICE.

Blind-Side Wedge

Level 3

Skills Developed   Ruck defence

Level   Beginner/Intermediate/<u>Advanced</u>/All

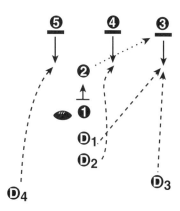

Explanation

This is a further extension of the front marker check and chase drill.

Player 1 plays the ball to 2 who rolls/passes in the direction of the first receiver (Player 3).

Once the ball has been passed/rolled, players 3, 4 and 5 (all carrying tackle shields) disregard it but advance as if ball carriers, Player 3 being first receiver, 4 being an inside receiver and 5 being a receiver attacking the 'belly' of the ruck area.

The front marker D1 checks the dummy half before chasing at the first receiver, while back marker D2 momentarily holds before following D1 and tackling Player 4 (the inside ball receiver). D3 (the first open side defender) moves up quickly to assist D1 tacking the first receiver. D4 (the first blind-side defender) makes his first movement forward before wedging in to tackle Player 5 who is attacking down the 'belly' of the ruck area.

Variations and Progressions

i) Practise to right and left.

ii) When competent play 6 v 6 grab in a restricted area 15m wide x 40m long.

Encourage the attackers to run from dummy half, switch the ball, play inside passes etc.

Coach the defenders so as to be able to deal with these situations, emphasising the marker system, the blind-side wedge and the open-side defence.

NB The above is for a front marker check and chase system. If you use a different system practise that by adapting the drill and its variations and progressions.

'Doubles' Defence

Skills Developed	Front marker system defence
	Blind-side wedge
	Communication

Level   Beginner/Intermediate/<u>Advanced</u>/All

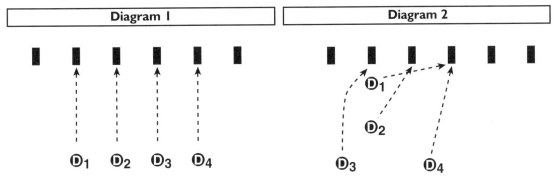

Diagram 1	Diagram 2

Explanation

Defenders line up as shown in Diagram 1 opposite six tackle bags.

All defenders advance and hit the bag opposite.

The coach calls out a defender number, e.g., 1.

The named defender takes up the front marker position where he tackled the bag, the nearest defender becomes back marker and the other two defenders take up positions either side of the ruck (see Diagram 2).

The coach should then indicate which way the chase has to go and the front marker should chase across two bags in that direction (as shown in Diagram 2) and effect a tackle.

The back marker should stand his ground initially and then take the inside bag (as Diagram 2) and effect a tackle.

The blind-side defender should wedge in and take the bag where the front marker had started from (as Diagram 2) and effect a tackle.

The open-side defender should assist the front marker in the tackle (as Diagram 2) as if wrapping the ball up and preventing a pass.

After this, each defender retires 10m and takes up a position directly opposite any bag.

The process then re-starts all over again.

It is recommended to complete six sets of double tackles as described.

Emphasise good technique.

Two Step

Skills Developed

Slide defence

Advancing before sliding

Level

Beginner/Intermediate/<u>Advanced</u>/All

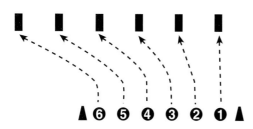

Explanation

A compressed defensive line (Players 1 to 6) line up between the markers.

On a given command the line advances quickly 'two steps' forward before sliding out on a man-to-man basis.

The defenders then hit the tackle bags with good technique before retreating back to their positions.

The drill continues for six tackles.

Variations and Progressions

i) Practise the slide to both right and left.

4 v 2 Cover

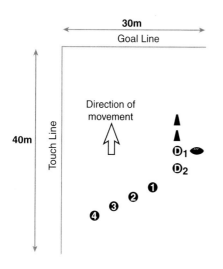

Skills Developed

Cover defence

Communication

Level

Beginner/<u>Intermediate</u>/<u>Advanced</u>/All

Explanation

Player D1 plays the ball to Player D2. Player D2 passes the ball to Player 1. As soon as this has taken place, D1 and D2 run around the cones and become defenders. Players 1 to 4 attack the goal-line.

NB It is recommended that a two-handed touch or grip is used.

Variations and Progressions

i) Different numbers of attackers and/or defenders.

ii) Size of the area.

NB The emphasis can be shifted on to the four attackers, making appropriate decisions to beat two covering defenders.

Slide Conditioned Game

Diagram I

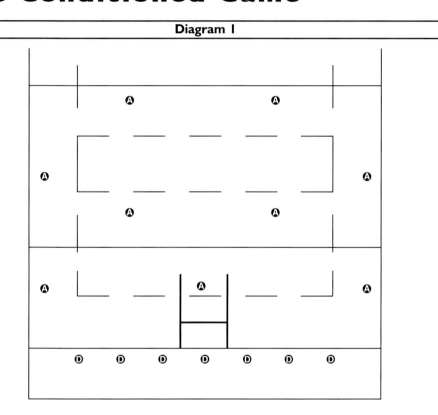

Skills Developed   Line defensive pattern
Communication in defence
Defensive decision making

Level   Beginner/Intermediate/<u>Advanced</u>/All

Diagram 2

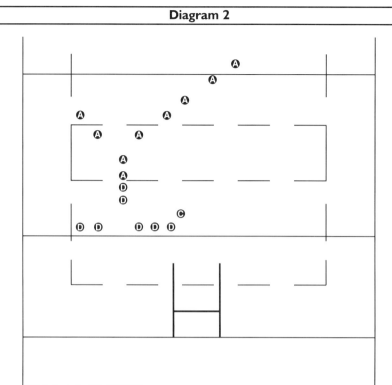

Explanation

A conditioned game using the sliding defence can be played in half the playing field.

Seven defensive players start from behind the goal-line, and the ball is drop-kicked out to the nine attackers (as in Diagram 1).

The nine attackers then have six plays to score a try – no kicking is allowed. In addition the attackers are conditioned to attack via wide plays on either open- or blind-side in order to try to out-flank the defenders.

The defenders are conditioned always to have two players at marker and to number off and equate numbers on the blind-side. This obviously leaves a short fall on the open-side and as the attackers will be trying to get around the outside of the defenders, the defenders will have to move up, communicate and slide.

The coach acting as referee should verbally control the play the ball so as to ensure the defence is set, while still keeping pressure on them. The referee should also set the defensive line and make sure all the defenders are inside of him make sure the line is tight or stacked near to the play the ball (as in Diagram 2).

NB It is recommended that a two-handed touch or grip be used for these practices.

Variations and Progressions

i) Change the emphasis in order to make it an offensive decision-making game.

Decision Making

The many skills and techniques of Rugby League have been discussed previously. Drills and small-sided games have been suggested for the players and relevant coaching points for the coach. Inherent within many of the activities has been decision making. This section of the book looks at what decision making is, and also at games specifically designed to emphasise this aspect of a player's development.

One of the most astute decision makers in the modern game, Shaun Edwards of Wigan and Great Britain.

Successful decision making is essential for the truly gifted performer and this process takes place in all game situations whether the player is advancing the ball, passing the ball, receiving the ball, supporting the ball, kicking the ball, chasing the kick, receiving the kick, in defence situations, etc.

In other words players are making decisions throughout the duration of the game, in every conceivable situation within the game.

A good decision maker is aware of the changing situation around him, i.e., the position and movement of team mates, the position and movement of the opposition, external factors such as the weather and ground conditions, game situations, such as the score and the amount of time left in a game. By correctly interpreting these stimuli the gifted decision maker will act accordingly.

In order for a player to develop the ability to be a successful decision maker he must be placed in many game-related decision-making situations through drills and small-sided games. Then, with direction from the coach, he must be encouraged to think for himself so that his decision-making ability is nurtured.

The following games have been specifically devised in order to emphasise the development of decision making.

Level 3

Corridor Rugby

Skills Developed   Contact evasive skills

Close support play

Decision making

Level   Beginner/<u>Intermediate/Advanced</u>/All

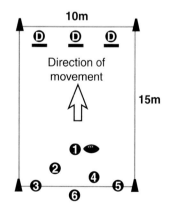

Explanation

In a corridor, as shown, six attackers have to advance down the corridor via determined running, good support and ball control in order to score a try.

The three defenders with shields attempt to force the attackers out of the grid and force an error.

If an attacker is grounded, he simply re-gains his feet and play re-commences with an onside pass.

When a try is scored, add a further defender until it ends with a 6 v 6 situation.

Ensure a different initial ball carrier each time.

Yardage

Skills Developed   Team control of the ball
Organisation
Close support
Decision making

Level   Beginner/Intermediate/<u>Advanced</u>/All

Explanation

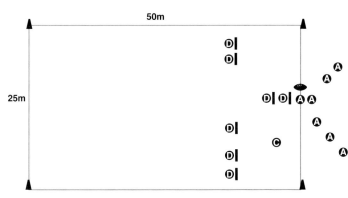

The playing area is set out as in the diagram. The attacking team (A) have five plays in which to advance the ball using previously worked dummy half plays. The defenders (D) have shields and attempt to prevent progress.

After five play-the-balls the distance covered is marked, the teams swap roles and the new attackers attempt to beat the first team's yardage mark. The coach (C) acts as referee, sets the defensive line, determines when the tackle is made and controls the speed of the play-the-ball.

Variations and Progressions

i) Two-handed touch or grip rather than a shield 'hit'.

ii) Emphasis on defensive organisation at marker, numbering off or wedge on the blind side.

Overload attack

Skills Developed   Passing and Handling
Decision making
Support play

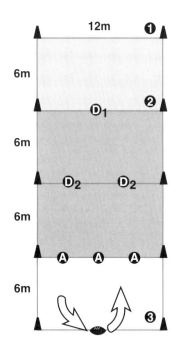

Level

Beginner/Intermediate/<u>Advanced</u>/All

Explanation

The game begins with the players positioned as shown.

On the coach's command the following happens: - attackers retreat to line 3, pick up the ball and begin attacking.

Defenders (D2) retreat to line 2, place their hands on the ground and become live defenders in the shaded area.

Defender (D1) retreats to line 1, places his hands on the ground and becomes a live defender in the top area.

NB

i) defenders can only defend in the designated area.

ii) a two-handed touch is used as a tackle.

Variations and Progressions

i) Defenders pick up shields and use these to defend with rather than a two-handed touch.

4 v 3 Floater

Skills Developed   Passing and Handling
Decision making

Level   Beginner/<u>Intermediate</u>/<u>Advanced</u>/All

Explanation

A1 starts in the end zone with the ball. As he has the ball he may enter the field of play so that the attacking

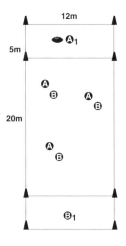

team has 4 players in field. The defending team (B) has 3 players in the field of play plus B1 who cannot leave the end zone.

The attacking team score a touchdown if an attacking player carries or catches the ball in the defenders' end zone. Passing is allowed in any direction. If the A team are attacking and make an error or have a player 'tackled', possession is handed over to the B team, B1 can then enter the field of play and A1 must return to the A team's end zone.

NB Two-handed touch is used as a tackle.

Variations and Progressions

i) Number of players and size of playing area.

ii) Passing restricted to technically correct Rugby League passing.

iii) Three 'tackles' allowed to afford greater ball control.

iv) Passing backwards only with Rugby League defence.

5 v 3 Counter Attack

Skills Developed
Support play

Passing and handling

Decision making

Level
Beginner/Intermediate/<u>Advanced</u>/All

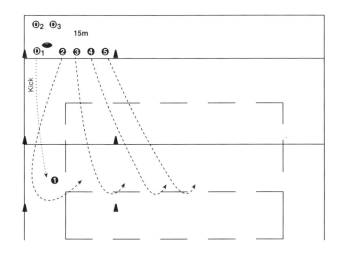

Explanation

Defender D1 starts with the ball and kicks it into the 15m grid where Player 1 is waiting. As soon as the ball is kicked Players 2, 3, 4 and 5 sprint to form a counter attack team attempting to score a try. Player 2 must run around player 1 as a winger coming around a full-back receiving a kick. Upon Player 1 receiving the ball D1, D2 and D3 become active defenders. A two-handed touch or grip is used and the full width of the pitch.

Variations and Progressions

i) An additional defender is added coming from the opposite corner.

ii) Can be used in a confined area for close support skills with defenders having shields and emphasising hit and spin, the bump off and off-load.

6 v 2/3/4/5/6

Skills Developed	Passing and Handling
	Decision making
	Control of the ball
	Support play
Level	Beginner/Intermediate/Advanced/<u>All</u>

Explanation

The game is played on half the full pitch.

Players are divided into two groups of six.

Six attackers spread out as if to receive a drop out from under the posts.

Two defenders drop kick the ball out to the attackers. If the ball goes out of play the attackers score one, i.e., the ball must come to rest in the half of the field being used.

The attackers upon receiving the drop out have six plays in which to score.

Normal rules apply except a two-handed touch replaces a tackle.

If the attackers score, the game restarts with 3 defenders and so on until it becomes 6 v 6.

If the attackers make an error, the teams interchange, i.e., attackers become defenders and vice versa.

Variations and Progressions

i) If required it may be necessary to allow the attackers up to 3 errors in the set of 6.

ii) If the major emphasis is on ball control a kick and prevention of the defenders coming out of their own in goal area when in possession of the ball should result in a further set of 6 tackles as in the full game.

Roll in

Skills Developed	Decision making in defence
	Communication
	Slide defence
Level	Beginner/Intermediate/<u>Advanced</u>/All

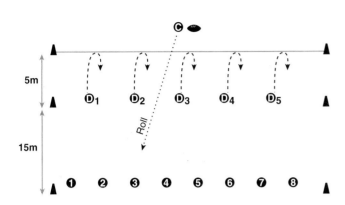

Explanation

Cones and players start as in diagram. The coach rolls the ball anywhere between the two sets of cones. Both defenders and attackers are facing the coach. When the ball is rolled players 1 to 8 react by retrieving the ball, playing it and attacking. The defenders on seeing the ball rolled sprint to the line before becoming alive. Defenders have to prevent a score by communicating and working as a unit as to the direction of the slide.

Variations and Progressions

i) Give the attackers 3 tackles to try to score.

ii) The emphasis can be shifted to attacking decisions in order to break down a slide defence.

Touch Rugby Variations

Skills Developed   Game related skills

Decision making

Level   Beginner/Intermediate/Advanced/<u>All</u>

Explanation

Normal Rugby League rules but a two-handed touch instead of tackling.

It is recommended that the maximum number per team is 9 and the playing area is amended accordingly.

Furthermore, in order to gain full benefit it is better to further condition the games to achieve specific coaching aims.

Variations and Progressions

i) One tackle touch.

As above but each team is only allowed one tackle at a time. Can be extended to two/three tackle touch.

ii) Three pass touch.

As above but three passes must be thrown every play-the-ball, otherwise a hand-over occurs.

iii) Over load touch.

As above but two players designated by the coach leave the field of play when their team is defending.

iv) Two ball touch.

As above but there is no six tackle rule. The game is played as normal except that at the coach's command the ball that is being used becomes 'dead' and must be placed on the ground.

The coach then introduces a second ball into play via a roll, pass or kick, and the first team to gain possession play on immediately towards their original goal-line.

There is no pause or stoppage. Teams have to react quickly.

The coach then recovers the first ball and continues to repeat this procedure at his discretion.

Possession Ball

Skills Developed   Passing and handling

Ball control

Decision making

Level   Beginner/Intermediate/Advanced/All

Explanation

Two teams 8 v 8 play touch rugby on a full-sized pitch. One team starts with the ball 10m from their own goal-line. Play the ball start from a central position. Unlimited tackles, the attacking team has the ball for a set time.

If the ball carriers make an error in their own half, they lose 8m of territory. If the ball carriers make an error in the opposition half, there is a 4m loss. Two-handed touch for the tackle.

The aim of the attackers is to score as many tries as possible in the time period.

After the set time period, reverse team roles.

Variations and Progressions

i) Defenders use shields instead of a two-handed touch.

ii) Different player numbers and pitch size.